PM+

Teachers' Guide

Levels 12–14

Elsie Nelley

NELSON

THOMSON LEARNING

PM Plus is published by Nelson Thomson Learning and is distributed as follows:

Nelson Thomson Learning

AUSTRALIA
102 Dodds Street
Southbank 3006

NEW ZEALAND
Nelson Price Milburn
1 Te Puni Street
Petone

UNITED KINGDOM
Thomas Nelson & Sons Ltd
Nelson House
Mayfield House
Walton-on-Thames
Surrey KT12 5PL

Email nelson@nelson.com.au
Website http://www.nelson.com.au

First published in 2000
10 9 8 7 6 5 4 3 2
07 06 05 04 03 02 01

Text copyright © Elsie Nelley 2000
Photographs copyright © Nelson Thomson Learning 2000

PM Plus Teachers' Guide: Levels 12–14
ISBN 0 17 009758 7

Edited by Jay Dale
Photographs by Bill Thomas
Illustrated by Boris Silvestri
Printed in Australia by DPA

Nelson Australia Pty Limited ACN 058 280 149 (incorporated in Victoria)
trading as Nelson Thomson Learning.

Acknowledgement
The publishers would like to thank the teachers and students at Broadmeadows Primary
School for their willing participation in the photographs used throughout this book.

Contents

What the PMs are about

The books in the PM Plus series have been written to complement the books in the PM Library and to be used alongside them. Like all the other PM titles, every aspect of the PM Plus titles has been carefully thought through and shaped to meet the developmental needs of young children who are learning to read.

The philosophy that underpins all the material in the PMs is based on the teaching and writings of Dame Marie Clay, the pioneering work of Myrtle Simpson and Pat Hattaway at the Department of Education, New Zealand, and Warwick Elley's research on words children use in their writing. The PM authors — Beverley Randell, Annette Smith and Jenny Giles — have brought their extensive, hands-on classroom experience in teaching beginning readers to the writing and final shaping of the books.

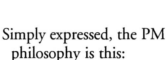

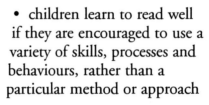

Simply expressed, the PM philosophy is this:

- children learn to read well if they are encouraged to use a variety of skills, processes and behaviours, rather than a particular method or approach

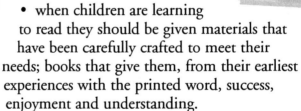

- when children are learning to read they should be given materials that have been carefully crafted to meet their needs; books that give them, from their earliest experiences with the printed word, success, enjoyment and understanding.

Every book in the PM series has been shaped to support these twin tenets. On every page in every book, care is taken with the sentence structures; the choice of words; the clear, well-spaced type; and with the meaningful, accurate illustrations. Because the books are easy as well as interesting, children are able to practise a variety of reading skills and enjoy the feedback of success.

Each PM Story Book has a classic story structure and deals with concepts and experiences children can understand. It is a real reading experience and has an intrinsic worth because it offers children a proper story structure with tension, climax and resolution. PM Story Books tempt children to reread. They want to revisit the text in order to recapture the success and enjoyment they experienced the first time the stories were read.

Some children prefer reading non-fiction. It fascinates them. In the PM Non-fiction titles the text is carefully researched, accurate and truthful in the way it deals with its subject matter. Clear and logical presentation of the facts, coupled with superb photography and realistic illustrations, make the books relevant, satisfying and enjoyable to read. A delight in truth and a respect for the real world in all its diversity are very much part of the PM meaning-driven philosophy.

All the PM titles have been written using carefully selected vocabulary. In each successive book in the series beyond Level 5, there is a very low ratio of new word introduction (at most 1:20). Each title is completely child-centred and full of meaning. Meaning is paramount in the PMs.

What are the skills, processes and behaviours children use when reading PMs?

The text, illustrations and page layouts of all the books in the PM series have been designed so that children can:

- develop the right concepts about print

- acquire a growing number of high frequency words (sight words)

- build and use a storehouse of known words

- use visual, syntactical and semantic cues to derive meaning from text

- apply reasoning and prediction skills

- link the reading and writing processes

- practise self-extending skills.

When beginning readers are being helped towards literacy, no one skill should be allowed to exclude the other important skills that are needed in the complex and multi-faceted task of learning to read. The PM materials allow children continual opportunities for developing the skills, processes and behaviours to become successful readers.

What is it about the books themselves that give children success, enjoyment and understanding?

1 Because success matters, a very **gentle learning gradient** or **levelling system** has been created. This is so that children are not confused by being asked to process too many unknown words on a page. Each book has been graded to avoid frustration-level reading, the situation in which a child makes so many errors that the meaning of the text is lost. The built-in meticulous levelling of a PM book gives teachers confidence that:

The same high frequency words will be reinforced in several books at the same and succeeding levels.

- new high frequency vocabulary will be introduced slowly

- the same high frequency words will be reinforced in several books at the same and succeeding levels

- text length will be appropriate for the reading experience of the young child

- skills can be introduced when developmentally appropriate

- language structures will match and extend the child's spoken and thinking vocabulary.

> Gran and Meg ran down the beach.
>
> "Gran! Look at this big rock!" shouted Meg.
>
> "It looks like an island!"

> Meg and Gran started to make a fence with sticks from the beach.
>
> But the bird was not happy. It still ran up and down and cried out. Its wings were down.

2 Illustrations should help children interpret the story and add to their success and understanding. Enormous care and attention is paid to the **close match of text and illustration** in a PM book. Writer's drafts are revised many times, artist's roughs are re-drawn and photographer's shots may be re-taken several times before the authors and publisher consider the books convey the essential meaning to the young child.

The illustration style is most often realistic, so that nuances of meaning and emotion can be portrayed in characters' faces and body language, thereby enhancing and giving depth to the child's understanding of the story.

Realistic illustrations enable characters' emotions to be portrayed.

> Hannah helped Alex to push the little bike over to her place.
>
> Alex showed it to Mum.
>
> "You are lucky," said Mum. "But let's put it in the shed. I don't want you to ride it if it's not safe. Dad will have a good look at it as soon as he can."

> The butterfly moved its wings again. But it did not fly away. It started to slip off the chrysalis.
>
> "Oh, no!" cried Anna. "The butterfly is going to fall."

> 'The reader needs the kind of text on which the reading behaviour system is working well... at the heart of the learning process there must be the opportunity for the child to use a gradient of difficulty in texts by which he can pull himself up by his bootstraps.'
>
> Becoming Literate: the Construction of Inner Control, *Marie Clay, Heinemann, 1991.*

Mother Duck walked down the hill.

Dilly Duck and Dally Duck ran after her.

Splash! Splash! Splash!

A specially modified font is used for the earliest books, and there is adequate space between letters, words and lines.

The mice raced over to the fence. Then they stopped.

"We can't get under there!" cried Grey Mouse.

"Now the cat will catch us and eat us," said White Mouse.

"We can get under the gate," said Brown Mouse. "Come on."

3 A specially modified font is used for the earliest books, and here the text itself is carefully positioned on the page to help young children with directionality. Adequate space between letters, words and lines is provided so immature eyes can see each letter and word clearly. Each line break and page break is carefully considered so that it contributes to the meaning of the story. Each serifed font used at a later level has been selected for its clarity and grace.

Why do children get so much enjoyment from reading PMs?

One of the recurring comments from teachers using PMs is that a child's first choice from a selection of books is often a PM Story Book. One of the reasons is that they know they will taste success, and that certainly contributes to their enjoyment. Without success, enjoyment of reading is impossible.

Sustained enjoyment comes from the readable text; the child-centred, high interest topics; the beautiful illustrations and the vital ingredient — a story line. Proper story structure puts life into the simplest of books by capturing and holding the reader's attention. Most children who are reading a story want to know what will happen next, so they continue reading to find out. They can empathise with the central character(s) and enjoy the satisfactory resolution on the last page. Without story structure, beginning texts become mere reading exercises.

No matter how long or short the story, or how many variations appear to be woven into it, each PM story follows the same traditional pattern — the central character(s) has a problem, and by the end of the book the problem is solved in a satisfactory way. This structure is detectable, too, in every

Proper story structure puts life into the simplest of books.

One day, after school, James went to play at Scott's house for the first time.

"I want to have a garden like yours," said Scott.
"But we don't have any room."

"Have you got a wheelbarrow?" said James.

"A wheelbarrow!" said Scott.
"No, we don't have one."

"You can make a little garden in a wheelbarrow," said James.

Scott's mother came out.

James said to her, "We have an old wheelbarrow at home. I will see if Scott can have it."

"Then I can make a little garden in it," smiled Scott.

"Thanks, James," said Scott.
"Now I have a garden, too."

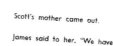

quality children's picture book. *The Very Hungry Caterpillar, Rosie's Walk, Harry the Dirty Dog* and all the timeless favourites such as *Cinderella* or *The Three Billy Goats Gruff* are written in 'story form'.

A story is a powerful way of delivering enjoyment, and always will be… and because stories are powerful they can 'hook' children on to reading.

A variety of lifestyles, families and ethnic groupings is evident in the PM titles.

Enjoyment comes from humour

Many PM titles bring a smile to children's faces with their gentle humour. Yet no character is ever laughed at or 'put down' in a PM story. The aim is to make children feel good about themselves, enhancing their self-esteem.

Enjoyment comes from an attitude of acceptance

The acceptance of all, and the variety of life styles, families and ethnic groupings in PM books allow every child to find a character with whom to identify — Aboriginal, African, Asian, Caucasian, Chinese, Hispanic, Indian, Polynesian, and of course, mixed ethnicity. Some children are shown in a family with two parents, some without a father, some without a mother and some without siblings. The role of grandparents in bringing up children is respected. Children with disabilities are shown winning some of life's battles. The portrayal of a balanced community is not contrived; it simply reflects the real world to which children belong, and so adds to everyone's understanding and enjoyment.

Max and the Bird House

A Friend For Max

Enjoyment grows when characters are loved — in all good literature characters are true to themselves

Many of the characters in the PMs appear in a number of books and their personal character traits are consistently portrayed in each. Children identify with particular characters and seek out stories at later levels about their favourites. Most of the stories are about real children and real-life events. They have a 'ring of truth' that everyone can identify with and enjoy.

The Big Bad Wolf

A very wide range of topics and genre helps to 'hook' more children into enjoyable reading

The topics covered in the PM books range from the familiar losing of a first tooth, having a birthday, going to school, winning a race, and teasing Dad. There are stories about familiar and unfamiliar animals, animated vehicles, dinosaurs and folk tales. Over 700 different titles cover fantasy, history, natural history, fiction, traditional tales, technology, verse, songs and plays. Children approach reading from many different angles. A wide variety of subject and genre provides a range of choices. This helps teachers to make the right match of book and child.

Reading for pleasure is the most empowering reading that a child does

Enjoyment is one of the intrinsic rewards of reading and good readers do a great deal of reading for enjoyment (which includes the re-reading of old favourites). They gain pleasure because they are good readers. But it makes them good readers, too… all that extra practice means that they have more and more successful encounters with print, and more exposure to known and almost-known words. When a strategy is applied to an unknown word, the sense of a half-familiar passage gives young learners immediate and helpful feedback. In an easy 'reading-for-pleasure' text, the child's mind can grip the main message even while puzzling out a new word or two and attending to visual clues. This ability lies at the heart of reading. Reading involves attending to several things at once, and it is only with easy, pleasurable texts that such behaviour falls into place.

Why is understanding so important? What has been done in the PMs to help children understand what they read?

Adults read for pleasure and information, and children's reading should have the same goals. 'Getting the words right' is a pointless excercise if the text has no worthwhile meaning.

When classic story structure is used, meaning takes over because these stories hinge on meaning. To understand the story, children have to experience the tension and anticipate that something is going to happen. A satisfying resolution to the initial problem helps children understand the story in a way that an 'up-in-the-air' ending or a 'twist-in-the-tail' ending never could. **The logic of the story line helps children understand.**

'Reading for meaning is paramount'

Developing Life-long Learners, *Margaret Mooney, New Zealand Ministry of Education, 1988.*

The **concepts** in first reading books **must be understood** by the very young if they are to become successful readers. If children struggle with obscure fantasy, or any subject matter that is beyond them, their understanding is lost. Without understanding there can be no self-correction. Obscure topics are excluded from PM Story Books.

Understanding is increased by carefully drawn illustrations and well-selected photographs that illuminate the text and deepen meaning for the viewer in all sorts of ways. **Insights come from viewing as well as reading.**

Understanding comes from scientific accuracy, too. Non-fiction should be as accurate as the author can possibly make it, but fiction, too, should respect accuracy. The animal stories that are included in the PM series are all based on the known behaviour patterns and habits of the animals. Even the bear family stories that are fantasy (signalled by their wearing human clothing) have a base of fact — real bears go fishing, like honey, hibernate and have cubs that climb trees. Much reference and research material are supplied by the authors to the illustrators so that all the books are as accurate as possible in terms of scientific detail, landscape, historical background and modern street signs.

The animal stories that are included in the PM series are all based on the known behaviour patterns and habits of the animals.

Meaning shapes every page, every paragraph, every sentence, every phrase and every choice of word. When a novice reader stumbles on a word or a phrase in the text it should not be because the text is awkward or inaccurate, or that it doesn't make sense. Prediction and self-correction, important reading skills, can only work where the text itself makes good sense. Meaning is embedded in every PM book, fiction and non-fiction.

Success, enjoyment and understanding make the task of learning to read worthwhile and help turn young children into self-motivating, self-correcting, self-extending achievers.

With over 700 books in the PM range, teachers have a core reading program for children in their first three years of school — material that will open up children's minds, challenge their thinking and stir their emotions.

The reading classroom

'At the beginning of schooling when children enter formal instruction the foundations of all their future interactions with education are being laid.'

Reading Recovery: A Guidebook for Teachers in Training, *Marie Clay, Heinemann, 1993.*

First teaching practice

Important guidelines for good first teaching practice include:

- early reading experiences where children's responses are accepted as important and worthwhile

- flexible approaches to learning that recognise individual differences

- sensitive observation and analysis of children's language, reading strategies, attitudes and interests

- precise knowledge and understanding of the reading process

- secure relationships between children, care-givers and teachers

- high expectations of the learner

- recognition and extension of the skills and language that children bring to school

- consideration and knowledge of children's home cultures

- access to quality resources.

An effective learning environment

'Good first teaching is the foundation of education and the right of every child.'

Guided Reading, *Irene C. Fountas and Gay Su Pinnell, Heinemann, 1996.*

An effective classroom environment encourages children to become involved in learning. The essential features of such a learning environment include:

- appropriate routines and programs that are learner-centred

- an emotionally secure climate

- a curriculum with high expectations for all learners

- programs which cater for children's differing needs and learning styles

- print-saturated surroundings where children are immersed in challenging, rewarding language experiences

- opportunities for children to learn and use their developing skills in meaningful ways

- regular feedback that is relevant, appropriate and positive, and where effort is valued

- effective use of classroom fittings and colourful displays

- space for group and class activities

- care-givers who feel comfortable in their interaction with the school.

What is a well-balanced literacy program?

A well-balanced literacy program involves children in reading, writing, listening and speaking. It encompasses a range of experiences and approaches that encourage children to take increasing responsibility for their own learning.

Key elements

Reading to children

Every day the teacher should provide opportunities for children to listen to interesting stories, poems, rhymes and songs. Encourage children to join in. They will gain a love of books and the rhythms of language from experiences with quality literature. When teachers read to children, they provide opportunities for children to experience texts that they are not yet able to read for themselves.

Reading with children

Gradually introduce new challenges to children through shared and guided reading experiences.

Shared book approach

The shared book approach helps children to learn about reading in a non-threatening situation. Usually this involves the whole class, but might also occur with small groups.

While reading with children, the teacher is able to offer support and demonstrate strategies of sampling, predicting, confirming and self-correcting. Shared reading can involve enlarged books, reading charts, songs or poems that are read aloud. Reading to and with children in these ways makes learning pleasurable and children are able to behave like 'real' readers.

> *A stimulating, carefully planned writing program is an essential component of a successful literacy program. Reading from texts that children have written and published links the reading and writing processes.*

Guided reading approach

The guided reading approach supports children in group situations from emergent to fluent reading levels. Small groups are formed because of a common purpose. The teacher guides children as they discuss and read a selected text.

Through guided reading, teachers can assist children to develop positive attitudes and appropriate strategies that lead to independence. During guided reading, teachers provide necessary support while children take increasing responsibility for their own learning.

Reading by children

Have children practise reading with quantities of easy-reading materials. This enjoyable, independent reading activity should happen daily, even at the earliest levels. Children learn to read by reading. Familiar texts lead to children developing an independent self-monitoring system. Children may choose from texts that they have read previously or from texts that the teacher has selected. At other times, they should be able to select personally from a variety of texts — both fiction and non-fiction.

Guided reading

Guided reading is the heart of a well-balanced literacy program for emergent to advanced readers. This approach supports children so that what they do today with the teacher's support, they will be able to do by themselves tomorrow. This is often called 'scaffolding'.

The purposes behind guided reading include:

- support for children as they actively reconstruct meaning by sampling, predicting, checking, confirming and self-correcting

- children experiencing a variety of different texts

- use of carefully selected texts for the teaching and learning of specific skills, reading strategies and fluency

- opportunities for children to become independent, confident readers

- support for children as they discuss, question, read and think their way purposefully through a text

- manageable challenges that encourage children to take increasing responsibility for their own reading of a text

- assessment of children's learning.

'The end point of early instruction has been reached when children have a self-improving system.'

Reading: The Patterning of Complex Behaviour, *Marie Clay, Heinemann, 1979.*

Guided reading leads children to become effective silent readers.

Guided reading enables teachers to:

- interact with a small group of children for specific instruction

- help children to read from a range of different texts

- provide successful reading opportunities to extend children's confidence and language

- use materials with sufficient challenges to increase a child's ability to process

- help children develop a self-monitoring system

- support children as they interact co-operatively with other children

- monitor children's progress frequently and provide constructive feedback

- observe children's understanding and reactions to different texts

- plan learning experiences using information from on-going assessments.

Key elements of a guided reading lesson

Before the lesson

Identify the objectives that the children will develop during the lesson, e.g. children will:

- respond to language and meaning in texts

- select and read for enjoyment

- read for information

- develop conventions of print

- use structural and visual cues to gain meaning

- read with fluency and phrasing

- use personal background, knowledge and experience to enhance understanding.

Choose the best texts to meet these objectives, for example:

- select texts with sufficient known words for children to construct meaning; preferably no more than one new word in every 20 running words

- expect children to read instructional texts with 90–95 per cent accuracy

- select texts challenging enough for children to use skills and strategies confidently as they develop a self-extending system

- select from a range of text forms with meaningful content or well-shaped plots

- select from a wide range of subjects

- select texts where the language is natural and easy to read (containing familiar sentence constructions)

- ensure that the texts have attractive, well-drawn illustrations that enable children to gain maximum understanding.

Identify the purposes for the reading, for example:

- to practise one-to-one word matching or another print convention

- to introduce, reinforce or extend skills or strategies

- to enjoy a story by reading for meaning

- to explore a particular type of text (narrative, descriptive, informative, etc.).

The lesson

Creating the atmosphere

This is the 'tuning-in' stage. It is the time when the teacher focuses children's thinking on the content, concepts or information in the text. At this stage, related language or exciting new vocabulary can be discussed, written on the whiteboard or acted out. In this way, new ideas become familiar and children's language is enriched.

Focusing on the text

This is an in-depth study of the text. The teacher directs questions and discussion to enhance meaning, and to meet the purposes of the reading. Children may be asked to read parts of the text, to answer teacher-directed questions or to clarify what has emerged in discussion. The teacher supports children as they use strategies to solve challenges in the text. The teacher may

intervene to show children how to take responsibility for gaining a deeper understanding of the text. As children become more fluent readers, they are able to read longer sections of the text and even whole stories to themselves.

After the lesson

Going beyond the text

In some lessons, the reading of the text is sufficient and requires no further consolidation activities. At other times, teachers may select language enrichment activities to enhance and extend children's experiences and understandings gained during the reading. These activities give children the opportunity to interact verbally and co-operatively in small groups. They will often extend children's thinking beyond the content of the text.

On-going assessment

Regular assessment of children's progress is an essential component of guided reading. The method and type of information collected will enable the teacher to plan

learning experiences that match children's needs. See also 'Assessment', pages 26–33.

Classroom organisation

Guidelines

- The teacher works with groups of six to eight children.
- The teacher works with the group for fifteen to twenty minutes.
- The teacher works with two groups daily.
- The children usually sit on the floor in a semi-circle in front of the teacher.
- The teacher selects the text carefully and plans how to present it to the children.
- The teacher provides sufficient books for each child to have their own copy.
- The teacher has a whiteboard or chart to enhance visual learning outcomes.
- The groups are usually selected by reading ability, but they may be based on interest or experience.
- The composition of the groups changes as children achieve at different rates.
- The composition of the groups change when different purposes for the guided reading are identified and planned for.

Planning

Classes may be organised into three or four guided reading groups. All readers benefit from regular guided reading instruction. This should take place twice a week. The lessons should take no longer than twenty minutes each. Included is an example of a teacher's daily guided reading plan.

Example of a teacher's daily plan

Date: 23 February

Reading to children

The Lazy Bear (Brian Wildsmith, Oxford University Press, 1973)

Reading with children

Shared text/s: *Stone Soup* (PM Library Traditional Tales and Plays Turquoise Level)

Objectives: •To exchange ideas and opinions through interaction with others.

•To enjoy reading and acting out plays.

Responding to the text/s: Discussions about the meaning of 'trickery' and applying it to personal reading.

Guided reading

Group: 1 (Sharks)

Text: *Brown Mouse Plays a Trick* (PM Plus Level 9)

Purpose: •To reinforce children's understanding of the meaning of 'trickery'.

•To use visual sources of information to check text predictions.

Creating the atmosphere:

Show the children a wind-up toy. Discuss the technology of wind-up toys.

Focus: Refer to *PM Plus Teachers' Guide: Levels 9–11*, p. 48.

Going beyond the text:

Discuss the humour of occasions when a trick is fun but not hurtful. Write the children's ideas on a chart. Have them write about their own experiences and add illustrations. Put the stories together to make a book.

Group: 3 (Dolphins)

Text: *The Ant and the Dove* (PM Plus Level 15)

Purpose: •To discuss how the characters portray human behaviour in order to interpret the meaning of the moral.

Creating the atmosphere:

Reread a simple Aesop's fable, e.g. *The lion and the mouse* (PM Library Blue Level). Discuss the meaning of the moral: 'One good turn deserves another.' Explain that the new story is also a fable.

Focus: Refer to *PM Plus Teachers' Guide: Levels 15–16*, p. 56.

Going beyond the text:

Using the sequence of events from the book, help the children to role-play the story.

Groups: 2 (Angelfish) and 4 (Stingray)

Independent reading tasks. Refer to *PM Plus Teachers' Guide: Levels 9–11*, pp. 22–25.

Targeted children/learning needs:

Group 1: Tim, Michael — revise verb endings

Group 3: Sally, Tye — reading for meaning

Assessment:

Zac, Georgia, Maria

Example of a weekly plan

Here is an example of a weekly guided reading plan for four different guided reading groups. A weekly plan may be organised around four days. This allows one day for the teacher to plan for a shared reading or an integrated language experience, and for assessment.

Key

GR — Guided reading with teacher   **BLM** — Blackline master
T's G L — PM Plus Teachers' Guide Levels

Groups	Monday	Tuesday	Wednesday	Thursday
1	• Revisit familiar books. • **GR** *Brown Mouse Plays a Trick*, T's G L 9–11, p. 48. • Revise consonant blends: gr, br, tr, pl.	• Write about occasions when a trick is fun but not hurtful. • Illustrate and read to a friend. • Select from independent reading tasks.	• **GR** *Kitty Cat and the Paint*, T's G L 9–11, p. 40. Reinforce punctuation and reading with expression. • Extend the story – write about what might happen next.	• Complete BLM 4, (T's G L 9–11, p. 41). • Listening post with taped instructional material from earlier levels. • Select from independent reading tasks.
2	• Independent reading. • Reading own anthologies. • Listening post with taped instructional material from earlier levels.	• **GR** *The Donkey in the Lion's Skin*, T's G L 12–14, p. 48. Encourage fluency and phrasing. • Make a mural of the story.	• Reread *The Donkey in the Lion's Skin* silently. • Write captions for the mural. • Select from independent reading tasks.	• Complete BLM 8 (T's G L 12–14 p. 49). Ensure children understand instructions. • **GR** *Snowball, the White Mouse*, T's G L 12–14, p. 40. • Dramatise the story.
3	• **GR** *The Ant and the Dove*, T's G L 15–16, p. 56. Look at letter clusters. • Draw pictures on cards that retell the story. Sequence the cards as the story is retold.	• Reread *The Ant and the Dove*. • Complete BLM 10 (T's G L 15–16, p. 57). • Select from independent reading tasks.	• Revisit familiar books and poems. • **GR** *Chooky*, T's G L 15–16, p. 44. • Write 'Who am I?' descriptions of the main characters.	• Reread *Chooky*, and other PM books about mother animals keeping their young safe. Write and draw ideas on OHTs to share with the class.
4	• Reread *Stone Soup*. • Make masks. • Practise the play ready to present to the class. • Select from independent reading tasks.	• Independent reading – library. • **GR** *The Mouse-deer and the Crocodiles*, T's G L 17–18, p. 70. • Children work in pairs to draw a large picture of their favourite part.	• Reread *The Mouse-deer and the Crocodiles*. • Complete BLM 16 (T's G L 17–18 p. 71). • Select from independent reading tasks.	• **GR** *The Mouse-deer Escapes*, T's G L 17–18, p. 70. Reinforce cross-checking strategies. Look at letter clusters. • See 'Going beyond ...', p. 70 for instructions on making a board game.

Using a PM Plus text

Each double-page spread in the PM Plus teachers' guides provides a teaching plan and accompanying blackline master. The following descriptions relate to the features found in the teaching plan.

Running words
The exact number of words in the book being explored (see page 29).

About the story
This section contains notes about the story content.

Creating the atmosphere
Before reading the book, the teacher needs to focus children's thinking on the content and concepts. Related language or new vocabulary can be discussed.

Focusing on the story — guided reading
This is the stage when the teacher facilitates discussion and guides the readers.

STORY BOOKS LEVEL

Running words: 205

The Bears and the Magpie

About the story
This is another story about the Bear family. Mother Bear takes off her watch before going fishing and places it carefully on a big rock. When she returns for it, she is very surprised to find it gone!

Linking with other PM books
Honey for Baby Bear   PM Library Blue Level
Baby Bear Climbs a Tree   PM Plus Level 9
Baby Bear's Hiding Place   PM Plus Level 10
House-hunting   PM Library Green Level

Creating the atmosphere
Reread *Baby Bear goes fishing* (PM Library Yellow Level). Discuss the actions that these fantasy bears use when catching fish.

Focusing on the story
- **Cover** Read the title and study the cover illustration. Recall and discuss other stories about the Bear family.
- **Pages 2–3** Discuss Mother Bear's reason for taking off her watch. Draw the children's attention to Baby Bear who sees where Mother Bear puts her watch.
- **Pages 4–5** Observe the magpie's interest.
- **Pages 6–7** Talk about the illustration. Ask 'Where is Mother Bear's watch?' Discuss what might have happened to it.
- **Pages 8–11** Discuss the dismay felt by the Bear family. Point out their facial expressions. Ask, 'How is Mother Bear feeling?'
- **Pages 12–16** Identify the magpie's nest in the illustration. Observe Baby Bear's astonishment and delight when he finds the watch!

Going beyond the story
- Provide a selection of pictures, photographs and books about magpies. List things that the children could find out, e.g. what magpies look like, where they live, what they eat, their habits, etc. Record the information on charts or in individual booklets.
- Encourage the children to talk about finding things in unexpected places! Record their ideas on a chart. Ask them to draw pictures to illustrate their ideas. Display these pictures around the chart.
- Have the children write about objects that are kept in safe places so that they can be found quickly.
- With the children list things that do or don't go in water. Have them explain their reasoning.

Developing specific skills
- Revise contractions: don't, I'm, It's.
- Scan words for digraphs: watch, fish, Then.
- Use voice intonation to enhance meaning, e.g. 'Oh, dear', 'I can see a **watch**.'
- Discuss adverbs: around, away, again.

Using the blackline master
- Discuss the similarity between the words in the boxes. Complete the first sentence together.
- Read the words in the second section aloud. Guess each new word from the illustration. Check to see it rhymes. Discuss how to write the new word.

34   *PM Plus Teachers' Guide: Levels 12–14*

Linking with other PM books
Titles from PM Library and PM Plus that link by theme or language structure to the text being explored.

Going beyond the story
Teachers may select from or adapt these language enrichment activities to meet the needs of their class. All have been designed to develop purposeful and stimulating language.

Developing specific skills
These are the focus skills to be taught. They are not intended to be taught in isolation, but rather in the meaningful context of the child's current reading.

Blackline masters
The blackline masters in the PM Plus teachers' guides have real purpose, engaging children in independent activities that increase their skills with language.

Before children begin work on the blackline masters, discuss the sheet with them to ensure they know what they are doing, why they are doing it and how they are to do it.

Independent reading tasks

While the teacher interacts instructionally with small groups for guided reading, other children may be directed to independent reading tasks. At the beginning of the school year, and regularly throughout the year, an effective teacher will develop routines that support independent activities. Hence, children learn to work independently while the teacher supports a group or groups for guided reading. Independent activities should challenge the children's skill development and support their progress in reading and language.

The teacher needs to ensure that children are familiar with the activities and classroom routines before they are expected to practise them independently.

Children should also be encouraged to read with a friend or in a group, as well as by themselves.

Task ideas

Teach the children how to:

- respond to a text already read, e.g. a language enrichment activity or a blackline master

- revisit familiar books (it is recommended that each child has their own box of independent reading texts)

- read 'big books' or shared reading materials

- work at set tasks that reinforce a shared reading text, e.g. by innovating the text, making a group mural, etc.

- read at the listening post
- use transparencies with an overhead projector
- read stories, captions and labels from around the room
- read poem and song charts
- read a variety of different texts from the classroom library
- research and record information

- read and write in the writing corner
- interact with other children using literacy tasks, e.g. word lotto
- complete reading activities, e.g. word building games, crosswords, language jigsaws, dictionary tasks, etc.
- practise and perform plays
- read published personal and class writing.

Organising independent reading tasks

Below is an example of a daily program chart organised for independent activities. The teacher makes name cards for groups and/or individual children. These are attached to the chart with Velcro. The teacher moves the cards to direct children to specific activities. Children soon become independent at identifying their daily programs. Allowing children to be responsible for their own program ensures that the teacher is not disturbed while working with a group.

Example of a daily program chart

Guided reading groups	Sharks	Dolphins
Directed reading activity	Angelfish	Sharks
Independent reading (library, own reading box, shared reading books, poem cards, a play)	Stingray	Angelfish
Writing centre	Stingray	Angelfish
Reading activities	Dolphins	Stingray
Published classroom writing	Dolphins	Stingray
Listening post /OHPs	Dolphins	Stingray
Computer software	Dan Georgia	Maria James

Teachers often use picture charts to help children be responsible learners. Here is an example of a classroom chart that helps children remember the independent reading tasks that they may select.

Example of classroom chart

Independent reading

Library

Own reading box

Poem cards and song charts
I like dolphins
I like fish
I like ...

Listening post

Overhead projector

Big books
Seven little ducks

Reading activities

Read and write in the writing centre.
How to begin stories
In the morning...
One day...
Before school...
After school...

Practise a play

Read published writing
My Dad

Computer

Assessment

'In complex learning, what is already known provides the learner with a useful context within which to embed new learning.'

An Observation Survey of Early Literacy Achievement, *Marie Clay, Heinemann, 1993.*

Assessment is a necessary component of a successful language program. During assessment, teachers collect information about children's previous learning, language acquisition, skills, understandings, attitudes and interests.

The purpose of assessment is always to improve learning and teaching, i.e. to plan for the child's learning and to improve the program that the teacher implements. Information for assessment should be collected during the daily program.

Assessment procedures

The procedures that the teacher uses to assess reading may include both formal and informal observations, for example:

- anecdotal records of observations

- listening to children retell stories

- responding to visual language — picture interpretation

- accurate reading records (see pages 27–32)

- language monitoring checks (see page 106)

- conferencing between the teacher and the child, especially to determine reading for meaning

- analysis of writing skills

- self-assessment (children can be taught to set goals).

For a detailed description of taking, scoring and analysing reading records, see An Observation Survey of Early Literacy Achievement, *Marie Clay*, Heinemann, 1993.

Reasons for assessment

The key reasons for assessment are:

- to know the child as an individual
- to identify what the child has already learned
- to identify what needs to be learnt next so that learning experiences match learner needs
- to give the teacher accurate information for organising an effective class program
- to identify the most appropriate approaches and resources for the learner
- to provide constructive feedback to the learner and care-givers
- to monitor progress over time
- to provide information about individual, class or school achievement.

Regular assessment

It is essential for teachers to reflect upon their teaching practices, program outcomes and learning environment. Regular reading assessment identifies:

- how effectively the child is developing a self-monitoring system
- the child's awareness that reading should make sense
- the cues that the child is using or not using
- the child's knowledge of print conventions
- the child's attitudes towards reading
- the child's self perception of himself/herself as a learner
- the child's interests

- the child's abilities with other language skills, i.e. writing, speaking and listening
- the child's rate of learning
- the child's level of independence or requirement for an intervention program
- resource availability and the effectiveness of approaches.

What is a reading record?

At the centre of effective assessment is the technique of taking a reading record. This observation records precisely what the child is saying and doing. It provides an accurate description of the strategies that the child uses when sampling, predicting, checking, confirming and self-correcting.

Many reading records will be taken of the child reading from seen texts. However, unseen texts should be used if the teacher's purpose is to assess the child's confidence and ability to use and integrate strategies independently.

How to take a reading record

Learning to take a reading record takes practice. The child needs to sit or stand beside the teacher. The text must be seen clearly by the teacher and the child. First, ask the child, 'What is this book about?' This 'tunes' the child into the reading. The teacher then records everything that the child says and does while the child reads the text aloud. The teacher does not prompt the child and remains objective throughout the reading.

'The reason for using a "seen" text for the instructional level record is that we want to see how well the reader orchestrates the various kinds of reading behaviours he controls, given that his reading is being guided by the meaningfulness of the text. The "seen" text ensures that the child understands the messages of the text and meaningfulness will guide the reading.'

An Observation Survey of Early Literacy Achievement, *Marie Clay, Heinemann, 1993*.

A reading record should not take more than ten minutes. It is suggested that a reading record should be between 100–150 words (this will be less for texts at the earliest levels). Recording is usually done on a standardised record sheet (see page 111 for a blank 'reading pro forma') or an exact copy of the text (see pages 107–110).

Conventions used for recording

- Mark every word read correctly by the child with a tick.

> ✓   ✓   ✓   ✓   ✓
> 3. Dad said, "Come on, Tom.
>   ✓   ✓   ✓ ✓ ✓   ✓
> We will go to the shops."

- All attempts are recorded by showing the child's responses above the text. Record as one error.

Child:	the	them
Text:	there	

- If the child self-corrects an error, it is recorded as a self-correction, not an error.

Child:	the	SC
Text:	there	

- If a word is left out or there is no response, record it as a dash and call it an error.

Child:	—
Text:	today

- If a word is inserted, record it and call it an error.

Child: ✓   ✓   ✓   ✓ now✓
Text: Dad said, "Come on, Tom."

- If the child is told a word by the teacher, record it with a 'T' and call it an error.

Child:	saw	
Text:	was	T

- If the child appeals for a word, the teacher says, 'You try it.' If the child is unable to continue, record 'A' for appeal and tell the child the word. Record this as an error.

Child:	saw	went	A
Text:	was		T

- Repetition is not counted as an error, but is shown by an 'R' above the word that is repeated, as well as the number of repetitions, if more than one.

> R   or   R3
> ✓   ✓
> was   was

- Use 'R' for repeats plus an arrow if the child goes back over several words or even back to the beginning of the page.

>   R
> ✓   ✓   ✓   ✓   ✓
> Dad said, "Come, on, Tom.

- If the child appears confused, help by saying, 'Try that again.' This is counted as one error only before that piece of text is given a fresh beginning.

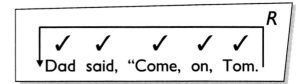

> ✓   some / sunny   ✓   TTA

Running words in the PM Library and PM Plus texts

In all PM Plus teachers' guides the number of running words for each text is indicated. Running words for the PM Library and PM Plus follow the rules listed below:

- the words on the cover and title page are not counted

- compound words are counted as one word

- hyphenated words are counted as one word

- animal noises that include a vowel, e.g. 'Baa-baa' are counted as one word

- sounds such as 'sh-sh-sh' are not counted as words

- numbers in numeral form, e.g. 1, 2, 3 are not counted as words, however when they are spelled out, e.g. 'one', 'two', 'three', they are counted.

Scoring a reading record

- The accuracy rate is calculated by dividing the number of words read by the number of errors. Table 1 (see page 30) will assist the teacher to calculate a percentage accuracy score .

- The self-correction rate is calculated by adding both errors and self-corrections together and then dividing by the number of self-corrections.

Analysing reading records

It is essential that the teacher analyses the behaviours that were observed so that the child's next learning step can be planned.

1 The teacher records each error and self-correction in the first two columns of the reading record (see page 32 for an example of a completed reading record). These errors and self-corrections are analysed further on the adjoining columns as:

- 'M' for the meaning
- 'S' for the structure of the sentence
- 'V' for sources of visual information.

2 The teacher analyses the child's behaviour before every miscue. When analysing self-correction behaviours, consider the miscue, then consider what extra information the child used to process the print. If the child has made no attempt to self-correct errors, identify if the child is:

- reading for the precise message, or

- is able to use cues effectively to monitor or problem solve, or

- has control of relevant oral vocabulary to read with understanding.

3 The teacher examines the analysis to determine how the child is responding to the different sources of information in the text.

A cumulative file can be kept of the child's reading progress. Ensure that any reading record kept for filing is dated with day, month and year. Include other forms of assessment such as annotated samples of the child's writing and oral language assessments, as well as reading records. Keep only useful information in organised files.

Analysing behaviours

To analyse the reading record, the teacher asks questions about these behaviours:

- Is the child competent with one-to-one matching?
- Does the child have consistent directionality?
- Is the child reading fluently at this level?
- When an unknown word is encountered, does the child:
  - make an attempt
  - make no attempt
  - seek help
  - re-run or repeat the word
  - read on
  - use meaning cues
  - use structural information
  - use visual information?

Table 1

Error rate	Percentage accuracy
1:100	99%
1:50	98%
1:35	97%
1:25	96%
1:20	95%
1:17	94%
1:14	93%
1:12.5	92%
1:11.75	91%
1:10	90%
1:9	89%
1:8	87.5%
1:7	85.5%
1:6	83%
1:5	80%

Scores

An easy text is 96% to 100%.

An instructional text is 90% to 95%. A text that is too difficult is 89% and below.

- When an error is made, does the child:
  - self-correct
  - ignore it
  - seek help
  - re-run or re-read
  - take the initiative to search further?

- When self-correcting, does the child:
  - use meaning cues
  - use structural information
  - use visual information?
- Which accuracy level is the child reading at?

Blackline masters

Reading record sheets

The PM Plus books, with their rich language structures and strong storylines, provide excellent material for monitoring children's control over meaning, language structures and visual information. 'Reading record' examples and a 'Reading record' pro forma (see pages 107–111) have been provided to assist teachers when analysing children's reading competence and skill development. These sheets are reproducible and ideal for the busy classroom teacher. An example of each story book at Levels 12, 13 and 14 has been provided and a non-fiction example has also been included to provide another opportunity for teachers to gauge children's reading skills. Procedures for administering and analysing reading records can be found on pages 27–31 of this book.

Example of a completed reading record

Reading record

Name: James   Age: 6.0   Date: 12/12/01
Text: The Fawn in the Forest   Level: 14   Running words: 111
Summary: James reads with fluency and phrasing. He often repeats a word, or reruns to the beginning of a phrase or sentence to check, confirm or self-correct. Needs to be extended to texts with more challenge. Accuracy 96% Self-correction 1:2

Page		E	SC	Errors MSV	Self-corrections MSV
2	A baby fawn lay hiding in the green forest.	1		Ⓜ Ⓢ Ⓥ	
	He lay in the leaves and the long grass				
	under the trees.				
	He lay in a secret place.				
	His mother had hidden him there.		1	Ⓜ Ⓢ Ⓥ	M S Ⓥ
4	The little fawn was all by himself.				
	He stayed very still.		1	Ⓜ Ⓢ Ⓥ	Ⓜ S Ⓥ
	The white spots on his back				
	looked like spots of sunlight on the leaves.	1		Ⓜ Ⓢ Ⓥ	
6	A fox came along.	1		Ⓜ Ⓢ Ⓥ	
	The baby fawn stayed very still.	1		Ⓜ Ⓢ V	
	He did not move his head.				
	He did not move his tail.				
7	The fox did not see the baby fawn,		1	Ⓜ Ⓢ Ⓥ	M S Ⓥ
	and it walked past.		1	Ⓜ Ⓢ Ⓥ	M S Ⓥ
8	A big cat came along.				
	The baby fawn did not move his ears.				
	He did not move his nose.				
	Totals	4	4	⑧ ⑧ ⑦	① ④

PM Plus Teachers' Guide: Levels 12–14   109

Language monitoring check

Regular monitoring of children's progress is an essential part of sound teaching practice. A 'Language monitoring check' pro forma (see page 106) has been provided to guide teachers' observations of children's reading and writing behaviours. It will assist teachers to monitor the language skills, understandings and behaviours of speaking, listening, reading, writing, viewing and presenting that should be developing at each stage of language acquisition.

Example of a completed language monitoring check

Language monitoring checks

Levels 12, 13 and 14
Skills, understandings and behaviours

	James	Michael	Ling	Amy	Brigette	Georgia		Date
Speaking and listening								
Speaks clearly and confidently on selected topics, maintaining the attention of the audience	✓	✓	✓	✓	✓	✓		¹²/₁₂
Clarifies or elaborates on ideas in response to questions	✓	•	•	✓	✓	•		¹²/₁₂
Reading and writing								
Uses appropriate reading strategies more frequently	✓	✓	✓	✓	✓	✓		¹³/₁₂
Reads for meaning and understanding	✓	✓	✓	✓	✓	✓		¹³/₁₂
Displays confidence in taking risks and making approximations in reading and writing	✓	•	✓	✓	✓	•		¹³/₁₂
Displays more skill in reasoning and predicting	✓	✓	✓	✓	✓	✓		¹³/₁₂
Displays increasing independence in reading a variety of books	✓	•	✓	•	✓	•		¹³/₁₂
Can read silently for a purpose	✓	✓	✓	✓	✓	✓		¹³/₁₂
Is developing expressive oral reading using punctuation	✓	✓	•	•	✓	•		¹⁴/₁₂
Can discuss book characters, scenes and episodes with understanding	✓	✓	✓	✓	✓	✓		¹⁴/₁₂
Can spell many words correctly	✓	✓	✓	✓	✓	•		¹⁴/₁₂
Makes logical attempts at spelling unknown words	✓	✓	✓	✓	✓	✓		¹⁴/₁₂
Is self-motivated to write often	✓	✓	✓	✓	✓	•		¹⁴/₁₂
Is beginning to reread own writing for meaning and spelling accuracy	✓	✓	✓	✓	✓	✓		¹⁴/₁₂
Viewing and presenting								
Finds and uses information from a range of sources, e.g. books, pictures, videos	✓	✓	✓	✓	✓	•		¹⁷/₁₂
Expresses feelings and ideas through different media, e.g. mime, movement, art, writing	✓	✓	✓	✓	✓	✓		¹⁷/₁₂

General comments (date all observations):

• *Demonstrate how to use information from texts when clarifying ideas in response to questions.*
• *Use both fiction and non-fiction texts in guided lessons.*
• *Emphasise expressive oral reading. Reinforce through role-play situations.*
• *Continue to provide additional opportunities at school and home of familiar reading texts for Michael and Georgia.*

The Bears and the Magpie

The Bears and the Magpie

About the story
This is another story about the Bear family. Mother Bear takes off her watch before going fishing and places it carefully on a big rock. When she returns for it, she is very surprised to find it gone!

Linking with other PM books
Honey for Baby Bear	PM Library Blue Level
Baby Bear Climbs a Tree	PM Plus Level 9
Baby Bear's Hiding Place	PM Plus Level 10
House-hunting	PM Library Green Level

Creating the atmosphere
Reread *Baby Bear goes fishing* (PM Library Yellow Level). Discuss the actions that these fantasy bears use when catching fish.

Focusing on the story
- **Cover** Read the title and study the cover illustration. Recall and discuss other stories about the Bear family.

- **Pages 2–3** Discuss Mother Bear's reason for taking off her watch. Draw the children's attention to Baby Bear who sees where Mother Bear puts her watch.

- **Pages 4–5** Observe the magpie's interest.

- **Pages 6–7** Talk about the illustration. Ask 'Where is Mother Bear's watch?' Discuss what might have happened to it.

- **Pages 8–11** Discuss the dismay felt by the Bear family. Point out their facial expressions. Ask, 'How is Mother Bear feeling?'

- **Pages 12–16** Identify the magpie's nest in the illustration. Observe Baby Bear's astonishment and delight when he finds the watch!

Going beyond the story
- Provide a selection of pictures, photographs and books about magpies. List things that the children could find out, e.g. what magpies look like, where they live, what they eat, their habits, etc. Record the information on charts or in individual booklets.

- Encourage the children to talk about finding things in unexpected places! Record their ideas on a chart. Ask them to draw pictures to illustrate their ideas. Display these pictures around the chart.

- Have the children write about objects that are kept in safe places so that they can be found quickly.

- With the children list things that do or don't go in water. Have them explain their reasoning.

Go in water	Don't go in water
• a boat	• a towel
A boat goes in water. It will float.	You cannot dry yourself on a wet towel.
• fish	• bread

Developing specific skills
- Revise contractions: don't, I'm, It's.
- Scan words for digraphs: wat*ch*, fi*sh*, *Th*en.
- Use voice intonation to enhance meaning, e.g. 'Oh, dear', 'I can see a **watch**.'
- Discuss adverb: around.

Using the blackline master
- Discuss the similarity between the words in the boxes. Complete the first sentence together.
- Read the words in the second section aloud. Guess each new word from the illustration. Check to see it rhymes. Discuss how to write the new word.

My name is _____

_____

around	away	again	about

This story is _____
three bears and a magpie.

A magpie flew _____
with Mother Bear's watch.

The three bears looked all _____
for the watch.

One day, Baby Bear saw it inside a nest.

Mother Bear will be pleased
to get it back _____.

_____

Make new words.

look cook _____

get met _____

all tall _____

can ran _____

see tree _____

top stop _____

A Friend for Max

About the story
The theme of this story has two strands: making friends and unselfishly helping a friend accomplish something they long to do. Friendship is a social skill that children will relate to with understanding when reading this text.

Linking with other PM books

Max and the Little Plant	PM Plus Level 8
Max Rides His Bike	PM Plus Level 8
Max Goes Fishing	PM Plus Level 8
Max and the Bird House	PM Plus Level 11

Creating the atmosphere

Reread *Max Rides His Bike*. Discuss the extra support that the trainer wheels provide.

Focusing on the story

- **Cover** Recall other stories about Max and Grandad. Talk about Max's need for a friend his own age to do things with.

- **Pages 2–7** Encourage the children to share their experiences of moving to a new house. Discuss the reason for Max's disappointment.

- **Pages 8–9** Invite the children to talk about what their families have done to welcome new neighbours.

- **Pages 10–11** Discuss friendships and how they develop.

- **Pages 12–13** Discuss Jake's caliper that gives extra support and balance to the leg that is weaker. Ask, 'Is there something that Max can do to help his new friend?'

- **Pages 14–16** The trainer wheels are like Jake's caliper — they give extra support. Discuss the satisfying conclusion.

Developing specific skills
- Discuss opposites: new, old; brother, sister; can, can't.
- Reinforce punctuation: quotation marks show direct speech.
- Recognise numeral names, e.g. six.
- Compare words with similar visual features: went, want; put, but; road, ride.

Going beyond the story

- Make a chart of different greetings, e.g. 'Hello', 'Hi!', 'Pleased to meet you', etc. Include greetings in other languages.

- Talk about how friendships develop. In pairs, have the children role-play some of their ideas. List the concepts that their ideas relate to, e.g. sharing, kindness, thoughtfulness, etc. Record the children's ideas on a chart. Have them write about their ideas. Bind the children's stories into a class booklet.

- Recall what Max and Grandad did to welcome the new neighbours. Have the children talk about what their families do to welcome new neighbours. Encourage them to write about these experiences. Present the children's work on a wall chart.

We invited our new neighbours over for a barbeque.
Ethon

Using the blackline master
- Discuss the words that the person with the speech bubble said at that time. Demonstrate how to find the required information in the story. Help the children to complete the first bubble together.

My name is _____

Max and Jake

About the story

This is a sequel to *A Friend for Max*. Children who have had to overcome a fear of water will empathise with Max's reluctance to go swimming. They will also understand his feeling of triumph when successful.

Linking with other PM books

Max Rides His Bike	PM Plus Level 8
Max and the Bird House	PM Plus Level 11
Come on, Tim	PM Library Blue Level
A Friend for Max	PM Plus Level 12

Creating the atmosphere

Reread *A Friend for Max*. Invite the children to talk about occasions when they have helped others to improve or learn new skills. Write their ideas on a chart.

Focusing on the story

- **Cover** Read the title together. Talk about Max and how he is feeling.

- **Pages 2–5** Discuss occasions when the children have invited friends to accompany them on an outing.

- **Pages 6–9** Observe Max's facial expressions. What do they tell the reader? Discuss why Jake might feel more competent and confident when he's in the water.

- **Pages 10–11** Talk about how Jake offers encouragement and advice. Ensure that the children understand that Max is still a little anxious.

- **Pages 12–16** Have the children search the text to find what Max did to help himself. Discuss his feeling of triumph and why Jake feels equally thrilled.

Going beyond the story

- Cut out a large circle from brightly coloured card. Around the outside of the circle, ask the children to write stories about helping others. Write 'We are helpers' on a smaller circle. Attach it to the centre of the larger circle with a split pin so that it can be turned as the stories are read.

- List skills or interests that the children could use to help others, e.g. using the computer, spelling new words, locating information in the library, etc. Put the list in a prominent place. Encourage others to use it when they need help.

- Talk about swimming activities that the children enjoy and swimming skills that they have mastered. Make an enlarged book of their ideas.

Developing specific skills

- Read *sm*, *sw* and *st* (PM Library Alphabet Blends books) to reinforce these beginning sounds.
- Discuss endings: ed — smil*ed*, lov*ed*, kick*ed*, help*ed*, look*ed*; ing — tak*ing*, swimm*ing*, hav*ing*.
- Discuss irregular past tense: swim, swam.

Using the blackline master

- Read the first sentence together. Talk about what the children will write and draw. Ask them to find the words they need in their books.
- On a chart, list the children's ideas on how they help at home and at school.

My name is _____

Max helped Jake.

He _____

_____

_____ .

Jake helped Max.

He _____

_____

_____ .

I help at home.

I_____

_____ .

I help at school, too.

I_____

_____ .

Snowball, the White Mouse

About the story

There is both tension and humour in this story about a little mouse who wants someone to buy him. The use of bold print encourages the children to read the text with emphasis and expression.

Linking with other PM books

A Party for Brown Mouse	PM Plus Level 8
Brown Mouse Plays a Trick	PM Plus Level 9
Brown Mouse Gets Some Corn	PM Plus Level 10
Pepper's adventure	PM Library Green Level

Creating the atmosphere

If possible (even for a short time), keep a pet mouse in a cage in the classroom. Discuss how to care for it. Read and discuss *Mice* (PM Library Non-fiction Orange Level) to the children.

Focusing on the story

- **Cover** Discuss the cover illustration and read the title. Talk about the types of toys pet mice are given and why.

- **Pages 2–3** Ensure that the children understand Snowball's fear of kittens and puppies!

- **Pages 4–7** Talk about Snowball's clever antics to divert the boy's interest.

- **Pages 8–11** Again, invite the children to respond to Snowball's actions.

- **Pages 12–13** Read the text with the children. Have them predict what Snowball might do in order to gain the boy's attention.

- **Pages 14–16** Discuss Snowball's actions. Enjoy the happy conclusion.

Going beyond the story

- Make fact books or charts about pet mice. These could be treated as individual projects that the children complete over several days. Talk about the essential information that would be included, e.g. what pet mice look like, where they live, what they eat, how to care for them, etc.

Some mice are white. Sometimes they are black. Sometimes they are black and white.

They have little bodies and long tails. They can run fast.

- Have a group of children dramatise the story. Discuss the characters in the story, the words that they say, and what the children need to do in order to accurately portray each character.

- Provide the children with a selection of construction materials, e.g. boxes, cardboard, cotton reels, netting, etc. Have them design and then make a cage for the two mice.

Developing specific skills

- Discuss compound words: someone, Snowball, inside.
- Revise pronouns: he, his.
- Discuss irregular past-tense verbs: hide, hid; run, ran.
- Talk about plurals: mouse, mice; puppy, puppies.

Using the blackline master

- Direct the children's attention to letters that are the same as they read each pair of rhyming words.
- Read all the sentences and select the appropriate missing words. Encourage the children to give reasons for their choices.

My name is _____

Snowball was a little white _____.

| mouse |
| house |

He did not like the pet _____.

| stop |
| shop |

He wanted someone
to come and _____ him.

| buy |
| fly |

A little _____
came into the shop.

| toy |
| boy |

He had a _____ mouse at home.

| black |
| back |

Snowball made the _____
go round and round.

| feel |
| wheel |

"I will buy you," said the boy.
"Then I will have two _____."

| nice |
| mice |

Look in the Garden

About the story

In this story, Scott goes home with James after school. He is horrified when James suggests they eat peas as an after-school snack. However, he is soon pleasantly surprised when he finds peas, fresh from the garden, are delicious.

Linking with other PM books

Sally's beans	PM Library Yellow Level
The best cake	PM Library Blue Level
Cows in the garden	PM Library Blue Level
The Wheelbarrow Garden	PM Plus Level 14

Creating the atmosphere

Show the children a packet of pea seeds. Talk about opening the pod to find the peas inside. If possible, give them an opportunity to eat peas straight from the pod.

Focusing on the story

- **Cover** Introduce the new characters, James and Scott. Read the title.
- **Pages 2–3** Establish that it is summer — the best growing time of the year. Name the vegetables growing in the family's garden. Have the children compare James's choice of an after-school snack with their own.
- **Pages 4–9** Ask, 'How do you know that Scott hasn't eaten fresh peas from a pod before?' Have them confirm their answers by reading the text.
- **Pages 10–13** Ask, 'What might James's mum say when she sees him eating peas?'
- **Pages 14–16** Invite the children to share doubtful feelings that they have had when trying something for the first time.

Going beyond the story

- Soak some pea seeds overnight and grow them on dampened cotton wool or in a miniature terrarium made from the lower half of a plastic drink bottle. Measure the pea plants regularly to see how far they have grown.
- Talk about gardens that the children are familiar with, at home and in the local community. Make a wall chart of their ideas.

My Grandma grows beans. I help her pick them. Kala

Sometimes we go to the Rose Gardens for a picnic. Jared

- Discuss occasions when the children have been doubtful about trying something new, and their opinions after trying it! Scribe their ideas on a large chart. Have the children draw pictures illustrating their ideas. Paste these onto the chart.

Developing specific skills

- Exclamation mark — revise the symbol, name and meaning. Read examples from the text.
- Make lists of words that rhyme: pea, sea, tea, etc.
- Revise contractions: won't, don't.
- Discuss adjectives before a noun: *little green* peas.

Using the blackline master

- Demonstrate how to search the text to verify the information in section one.
- Have the children place a tick or a cross beside the vegetables they like/dislike.
- Encourage the children to draw the vegetables they like.

My name is _____

Put **yes** or **no** in the boxes.

After school, Scott went home with James. ☐

James said, "Let's eat some beans." ☐

The boys went into the garden. ☐

Scott looked at the little green peas. ☐

Then Scott's dad came to get him. ☐

"I like eating new green peas," said Scott. ☐

Do you like these vegetables?   ✓   ✗

peas ☐

corn ☐

carrots ☐

tomatoes ☐

Draw some vegetables that you like.

The Jungle Frogs

About the story
This is a narrative with factual information about a rare species of jungle frog. It explains how the male frog builds a fence around the pool in which the female frog lays her eggs. This is not a common practice for most frogs.

Linking with other PM books
The duck with a broken wing	PM Library Blue Level
The Swan Family	PM Plus Level 10
The clever penguins	PM Library Green Level
Ten little garden snails	PM Library Green Level

Creating the atmosphere
Show the children photographs or illustrations of the life cycle of a frog. Invite those children who know about frogs to share their knowledge.

Focusing on the story
- **Cover** Discuss the cover illustration. Inform the children that jungle frogs climb trees and lay their eggs in rivers. Explain that the facts throughout this story, and the environment and the colouring of the frogs, are accurate.
- **Pages 2–3** Identify Mother Frog who is slightly smaller and a shade paler. Ensure that the children understand that solving the problem of finding 'a safe place' for the eggs, and later for the young tadpoles, is the focus of the story.
- **Pages 4–9** Discuss Father Frog's solution to the problem. Observe how he smoothes the mud on the fence with his wide, spatula-like fingers.
- **Pages 10–16** Talk about the improved chances of survival for the young tadpoles

through this ingenious solution to the problem.

Going beyond the story
- Set up an aquarium. Place some young tadpoles in it for the children to observe.
- Provide selected photographs and books that reinforce the life history of the frog. Help the children to search for relevant information. Ask them to record the life history on charts, using both diagrams and captions.
- Reread other PM books about animals that lay eggs, e.g. *Can you see the eggs?* (PM Library Starters Two). Discuss actions taken by the parents to protect their eggs.

Snails lay eggs.
They live in dark, damp places
and hide their eggs
under the ground.

Developing specific skills
- Revisit pronouns: he, his, him, she, her.
- Discuss the comparative: big, bigger.
- Compare the visual features of 'around' and 'round'.
- Find words in the text that rhyme with: cake, school, got, sand, day.

Using the blackline master
- Read the words and the sentences. Have the children select the appropriate word.
- Discuss water safety and why a pool needs a safety fence.

My name is _____

_____

| can | | can't |

"I _____ find a safe place
to lay my eggs," said Mother Frog

"I _____ make a little pool
with a wall of mud around it."

Mother Frog said, "I like this pool.
The fish _____ swim over it.

Now I _____ lay my eggs."

_____

Draw a swimming pool with a fence around it.

The fence will _____

_____.

Jordan's Football

About the story
This first book about Jordan and Kris centres on a bullying incident. Children who have experienced similar tactics will understand Jordan's dilemma. Authenticity is enhanced by the use of the present tense.

Linking with other PM books

Football at the park	PM Library Yellow Level
Sally's friends	PM Library Blue Level
Sam Plays Swing Ball	PM Plus Level 9
Billy at School	PM Plus Level 9

Creating the atmosphere

Discuss some of the bullying situations that the children have experienced. Talk about actions that they could take to resolve such situations.

Focusing on the story

- **Cover** Introduce Jordan and Kris. Discuss the cover illustration and the game they are playing.

- **Pages 2–3** Talk about how parks have spaces for children to play. Reinforce the important supervision that an adult or older family member provides.

- **Pages 4–5** Ask the children to predict the actions of the older boy.

- **Pages 6–11** Have the children comment on the actions, body language and feelings portrayed by the main characters. Point out that although Jordan is looking upset, he is still standing up for himself.

- **Pages 12–16** Discuss the relief felt by the younger boys when the joggers came

closer. Talk about how quickly the 'bullies' ran off when they realised Jordan's dad really was near!

Going beyond the story

- Reread the story, drawing the children's attention to the dialogue between the characters. Paint a park background on a large piece of paper. Ask the children to draw the events of the story on smaller pieces of paper. Paste these onto the background. Help the children write the dialogue between the characters in speech bubbles.

- In pairs, invite the children to role-play possible bullying situations. Use these situations to talk about different types of bullying tactics, and discuss how the children should best respond to them.

Developing specific skills
- Revise contractions: I'm, I'll, let's, that's, can't, he's, Don't.
- Revise adverbs: away, around.
- Discuss possessive apostrophes: Jordan's dad, dad's friends.
- Revise verb endings: ed — laughed, kicked, called.

Using the blackline master
- Have children find examples of contractions in their books.
- Complete the first sentence together.
- Have the children draw the big boy running off with his friends.

My name is _____

| Let's | I'm | Don't | That's |

Jordan's dad said,

"_____ going for a run around the park."

Jordan and Kris played with the ball.

A big boy got the ball.

"_____ go and play with this ball,"
he said to his friends.

Jordan said, "_____ my football
and my dad is here, too.

"_____ play tricks," said the big boy.

Turn this page over. Draw a picture of the big boy
running off with his friends.

The Donkey in the Lion's Skin

About the story

By examining the behaviours of the animals in this Aesop's fable, readers will infer, 'Its much better to be yourself, than to be a donkey and try to be someone that you're not.'

Linking with other PM books

The lion and the rabbit	PM Library Blue Level
The House on the Hill	PM Plus Level 10
The lion and the mouse	PM Library Blue Level
The Crow and the Pot	PM Plus Level 13

Creating the atmosphere

Reread *The lion and the mouse*. Discuss the behaviours of the main characters. Link their behaviours to the moral, 'If you're kind to others they will be kind to you.'

Focusing on the story

- **Cover** Discuss the cover illustration and read the title.

- **Pages 2–5** Talk about the donkey pretending to be something that he is not. Predict what he might do.

- **Pages 6–7** Compare the donkey's behaviour with teasing (i.e. playful and fun with no malicious intent).

- **Pages 8–11** Discuss the consequences of the donkey's actions. Talk about how the other animals must be feeling.

- **Pages 12–13** Do the children realise that the donkey has identified himself?

- **Pages 14–16** Discuss how the animals felt when they knew that they had been fooled. Help the children to parallel the behaviours of the animals with the way people might behave.

Developing specific skills

- Discuss the possessive apostrophe: lion's skin.
- Revisit plurals: monkey, monkeys; fox, foxes.
- Discuss voice intonation to enhance meaning, e.g. 'Hee-haw!'

Going beyond the story

- Discuss the actions and dialogue between the characters in the story. Have the children make character masks (refer to *PM Traditional Tales and Plays Teachers' Guide Purple Level*, pages 20–32 for mask templates). Invite the children to wear their masks as they dramatise the fable.

- Demonstrate how to write a simple book review.

- Make a mural of the story. Add different textured materials to the background. Have the children write captions describing the events in the story. Paste these onto the mural.

Using the blackline master

- Ensure that the children refer to their texts as they sequence the events in the story.
- Invite the children to add matching pictures.

My name is _____

The donkey ran after _____.

The donkey ran after _____.

The donkey ran after _____.

The zebras and the foxes and the monkeys ran after _____.

Running words: 222

The Lost Keys

About the story
This story is a sequel to *Teasing Dad*. It reinforces the importance of keeping keys in safe places. It offers opportunities for the children to discuss the plot, characters and sequence of events.

Linking with other PM books
Locked Out	PM Library Blue Level
Teasing Dad	PM Library Blue Level
The flood	PM Library Green Level
After the flood	PM Library Green Level

Creating the atmosphere
Reread *Teasing Dad*. Explain that the new book is a continuation of this story.

Focusing on the story
- **Cover** Read the title together. Discuss the real-life dilemma of lost car keys! Talk about trying to find the keys in the sand at the beach.
- **Pages 2–5** Check the illustrations to confirm that the family is only now leaving the beach. Discuss Dad's use of the word 'Sorry'.
- **Pages 6–9** Observe the sandcastle's changed shape. Discuss the movement of the waves as the tide comes in.
- **Pages 10–11** Observe Rachel's expression — it's been a long day, and she doesn't feel like looking for the lost car keys!
- **Pages 12–16** Discuss how the keys might have fallen into the water and how lucky the family was that Rachel found them. Examine Dad's body language on page 16.

Going beyond the story
- Show the children a selection of keys that are no longer in use. Have each child feel them and observe their different shapes. Discuss what each key might be used for. Make a concertina chart of the children's ideas.

- Talk about keeping keys in safe places and the unfortunate consequences if they are lost. Provide the children with paper shaped like a key and have them write about their experiences.
- Write a different ending to the story. Reread *The Lost Keys* to the end of page 10 and discuss with the children alternative solutions. Write each solution onto a sheet of paper. Have the children copy their preferred ending onto acetate transparencies or cards.

Developing specific skills
- List words that rhyme with: hill, by, sand, wave, now, feet, take.
- Revise compound words: sand/castle.
- Discuss verb endings: come, coming, came.
- Revisit 'y' endings: sorry, lucky.

Using the blackline master
- Read the verbs in the boxes. Demonstrate 'cloze procedure'. Remind the children to check for meaning.
- Revise words that rhyme. Look for a word that rhymes with 'will' on page 7. Ask the children to find the other rhyming words in their texts.

My name is _____

| laughed | looked | splashed | shouted |

Rachel and Sam went back to the beach.

They _____ for the car keys.

Rachel _____ in the waves.
She looked down at the wet sand.

"I can see the keys!" _____ Rachel.

"You can look after the keys," _____ Dad.

get   wet   no   go

will   _____   day   _____

and   _____   meet   _____

it   _____   not   _____

he   _____   can   _____

The Picnic Boat

About the story
When Rosie and Dad went fishing, they thought they had everything they would need — until they discovered that their fishing rods were still in the car! This text encourages the use of punctuation cues.

Linking with other PM books

Down by the Sea	PM Plus Level 11
A Treasure Island	PM Plus Level 11
The Naughty Ann	PM Library Green Level
The island picnic	PM Library Green Level

Creating the atmosphere

Encourage those children who have been fishing to share their experiences. If possible, show them a fishing rod and demonstrate how to attach bait to the hook.

Focusing on the story

- **Cover** Read the title together. Discuss the word 'picnic' and what it means to the children.

- **Pages 2–7** Revisit the children's understanding of water- and boat-safety practices. Ask, 'Do you think Rosie and Dad have forgotten anything?' Are the children anticipating what might happen?

- **Pages 8–11** Notice that Dad sits in the stern controlling the motor while Rosie sits safely on the seat in front of him. Later, he moves to the bow before letting the anchor down. Rosie's position has also changed. Discuss these safety practices.

- **Pages 12–15** Encourage the children to use intonation and expression when reading these pages.

- **Page 16** Talk about being forgetful, then having the outcome turn into a fun occasion.

Going beyond the story

- Provide the children with boat-shaped paper and have them write about something that happened in the story. Paste these onto a seascape background. Ask the children to draw Rosie and Dad wearing their life jackets and hats. Cut these out and paste them 'into' the 'dinghys'.

- Write Level 12 high frequency words on fish-shaped cards and attach a paper clip to each. Tie a small magnet to a piece of string. Have the children 'fish' with the magnet. When a 'fish' is caught, have the children read the word aloud. When all the words have been 'caught', count the number of words that were recognised.

Developing specific skills
- Revise endings: er — wat*er*.
- Discuss similarities and differences between pairs of words: bait, boat; basket, jacket; fast, first.
- Revisit the names for the days of the week.
- Discuss contractions: can't, let's.

Using the blackline master
- Reinforce the importance of meaning cues and visual cues when searching for information.
- Discuss ideas for the second part of the blackline master. Have the children check that all meaning cues are included in their illustrations.

My name is _____

_____

Rosie and Dad went fishing.

They took a _____,

a _____,

two _____,

and _____.

They forgot to take the _____.

We went for a picnic

We took _____

_____.

This is my picnic.

Sam's Haircut

About the story

Sam is reluctant to have her hair cut until her teacher arrives at the same salon to have her hair cut, too. The familiar context of this story encourages children to relate their own experiences to what they read.

Linking with other PM books

The Hairdresser	PM Library N. F. Blue Level
The Sam character series	PM Plus Levels 3–10

Creating the atmosphere

Read *The Hairdresser*. Encourage the children to share their own experiences of visiting the hairdresser.

Focusing on the story

- **Cover** Read the title. Identify Sam. Discuss the woman and who she might be.

- **Pages 2–5** Talk about the illustrations before reading the text. Read with the appropriate intonation and expression. Ask the children to share their own experiences at the hairdresser.

- **Pages 6–7** Have the children search the text for the reasons why Sam did not want to have her hair cut.

- **Pages 8–13** Talk about Sam's thoughts when she opens her eyes. Ask, 'Is Sam happy with her haircut?'

- **Pages 14–16** Have the children read the text to find out why Sam's teacher is visiting the hairdresser. Discuss the reasons for Sam's changed attitude.

Going beyond the story

- Invite the children to write about Sam's experience at the hairdresser as if they were Sam retelling it as class news. Demonstrate how to write in the first person.

- Have the children list the procedures for having a haircut. Ask them to search *Sam's Haircut* and *The Hairdresser* for words they might need. Invite them to check that they have included everything by reading their completed lists to friends.

- Talk about occasions when the children have happened to meet their teachers in places other than at school. Ask them to write about these times. Remind them that their statements should explain: when, who and where. Collate the stories into a class booklet.

Developing specific skills

- Use *cl*, *st*, *fl* and *sm* (PM Library Alphabet Blends books) to assist with the words: *cl*imb; *st*ill, *st*arted; *fl*oor; *sm*iled.
- Recognise opposites: long, short; do, don't; can, can't; will, won't.

Using the blackline master

- Read pages 4–5 in the text. Discuss what Sam did after school in the story.
- Talk about what the children do after school and write their ideas on a chart.
- Explain how to complete the blackline master.

My name is _____

_____

After school,

Sam _____

_____ .

After school,

I _____

_____

_____ .

After school,

I _____

_____

_____ .

Little Chimp and the Termites

About the story

In this factual science book written in story form, Mother Chimp successfully teaches Little Chimp a lesson on how to survive in the wild. The repetition of events in this story, encourages the discussion of language patterns.

Linking with other PM books

Little Chimp and the Bees	PM Plus Level 9
Bugs for Breakfast	PM Plus Level 9
Little Chimp and Baby Chimp	PM Plus Level 10
Mother Tiger and her Cubs	PM Plus Level 11

Creating the atmosphere

Read pages 12–15 of *Monkeys and Apes* (PM Library Non-fiction Turquoise Level). Explain that termites are very little insects that can be very destructive to trees.

Focusing on the story

- **Cover** Recall other stories about the Chimp family. Explain that the termite home looks like a 'brown hill'.

- **Pages 2–3** Observe that the 'brown hill' is a termite mound. Explain briefly what goes on inside such a mound.

- **Pages 4–9** Ensure that the children understand that Mother Chimp is teaching Little Chimp an important lesson. Observe how intently he watches her. Talk about what might happen inside the termite mound while Mother Chimp sits very still.

- **Pages 10–11** Discuss Little Chimp's imitation of Mother Chimp's behaviour. Talk about imitation as a means of learning new skills. Predict what he will do next.

- **Pages 12–16** Have the children read these pages independently to check their predictions.

Going beyond the story

- Reread other stories about the Chimp family (PM Plus Levels 3, 4, 6, 9 and 10). Discuss the different lessons that Little Chimp has learned in these stories. Write about the lessons on separate pieces of paper. Ask the children to add illustrations. Collate the sheets to make a class book.

- Demonstrate how to list the procedures that Mother Chimp followed to catch some termites. Invite the children to list the procedures followed by Little Chimp. Ask them to draw diagrams beside each procedure.

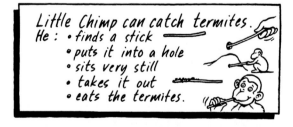

Little Chimp can catch termites.
He : • finds a stick
• puts it into a hole
• sits very still
• takes it out
• eats the termites.

Developing specific skills

- Revise capital letters at the beginning of names.
- Compare the letter-sound relationships in: *there, that, they, this.*
- Introduce the adverb 'very': *very* good, *very* still.
- Revise words that begin like 'along': *away, again.*

Using the blackline master

- Have the children retell the procedures Mother Chimp followed to catch some termites.
- Read the blackline master together. Ask the children to use their books to find the missing words.
- Discuss what Little Chimp did to help himself.

My name is _____

On day, Mother Chimp
went _____ the forest.

Little Chimp _____ along, too.

They saw a brown hill with _____
tiny holes in it.

Mother Chimp _____ a stick
into one of the tiny holes.

She put it down a tunnel.

She sat very _____.

She took the stick out.

It had _____ termites on it.

She gave one to Little Chimp.

He put the termite into _____ mouth.

It was very good to _____.

Turn this page over.
Draw a picture of Little Chimp trying to get some termites.

Three Little Mice in Trouble

About the story
Once again Brown Mouse cleverly initiates a plan to escape from the cat, only to find another problem has to be solved if the mice are to get home safely. Prediction and confirmation are components of this dramatic story.

Linking with other PM books
A Party for Brown Mouse	PM Plus Level 8
Brown Mouse Plays a Trick	PM Plus Level 9
Brown Mouse Gets Some Corn	PM Plus Level 10
Snowball, the White Mouse	PM Plus Level 12

Creating the atmosphere
Reread *Brown Mouse Gets Some Corn*. Talk about how the presence of the cat and the dog add tension to the story.

Focusing on the story
- **Cover** Read the title and discuss the illustration. Have the children recall other stories where the three mice feature.

- **Pages 2–3** Observe the cat as it comes across the lawn. Ask the children what they think might happen.

- **Pages 4–7** Study the illustrations. Note that the gap under the fence is too small for the mice to run under. Discuss how it is always Brown Mouse who quickly solves each problem.

- **Pages 8–11** Ensure that the children read with appropriate intonation.

- **Pages 12–16** Demonstrate how the handle of the latch opens the gate. Discuss the ending and how the mice feel relieved now that they are safe.

Going beyond the story
- Have the children reread other PM Library and PM Plus books about animals being chased by a dog, e.g. *Clever Fox* (PM Plus Level 6), *The duck with a broken wing* (PM Library Blue Level), *Little White Hen* (PM Plus Level 8) and *Brown Mouse Gets Some Corn*. Discuss the problems that the dogs initiate. Write the children's ideas on a chart. Add illustrations.

- With the children, brainstorm everything they know about gates — their construction, purposes, etc. Have them record and illustrate their ideas.

> We have a big gate. It is made out of wood. It stops our dog, Jake from running onto the road.
>
> My dad sells cars. Every night he locks the gate so no one can steal the cars.

- Provide small booklets and have the children write the story in their own words. This may take more than one day.

Developing specific skills
- Discuss and practise expressive oral reading skills (enhanced by the use of punctuation cues).
- Revise verb tenses (regular verbs): race, raced; smile, smiled; open, opened.
- Revise verb tenses (irregular verbs): come, came; run, ran; see, saw.

Using the blackline master
- Ask the children to read the words in the boxes and listen to the final sounds. Observe the common spelling of these endings.
- Read the words. Discuss the spelling patterns that the children will follow.

My name is _____

| smiled | opened | cried | raced |

The three mice got under the gate.

"The cat can't get us now,"
_____ Brown Mouse.

"We are all safe."

"No! Here comes the dog!" _____
White Mouse.

The little mice _____ up to the top
of the gate.

Up went the latch, and the gate _____.

Make new words. Read them to a friend.

play   playing   played

laugh   _____   _____

climb   _____   _____

help   _____   _____

The Crow and the Pot

About the story

In this Aesop's fable, a thirsty crow finds some water in a discarded pot but is unable to get his head inside. The scientific accuracy and logic of this narrative encourages the children to read for pleasure as well as information.

Linking with other PM books

The lion and the rabbit	PM Library Blue Level
The lion and the mouse	PM Library Blue Level
The Donkey in the Lion's Skin	PM Plus Level 12

Creating the atmosphere

Partly fill a selection of plastic containers with water. Discover that water levels will rise when displaced by solid materials, e.g. metal, concrete, stone, clay, etc.

Focusing on the story

- **Cover** Read the title. Observe the Greek pot. Notice the narrow neck.

- **Pages 2–3** Discuss how the illustration depicts a very hot and dry environment. Ensure that the children understand that the crow is a 'big bird'.

- **Pages 4–7** Observe how the crow inspects the inside of the pot by putting his head on one side. Predict what will happen next.

- **Pages 8–11** Have the children check their predictions before anticipating what the crow will do with the stones.

- **Pages 12–16** Talk about the water rising only a 'little way' with each stone. Admire the crow's determination.

Developing specific skills

- Discuss two adjectives before a verb: *very hot* day, *big black* bird.
- Identify words with blends: *crow, plop, black, stones, flew, tree, drink.*
- Revise irregular verbs: fly, flew; make, made.

Going beyond the story

- Let the children experiment further with the containers and solid materials used during 'Creating the atmosphere'. Have them write down their discoveries.

- Invite the children to make a model of the Greek pot with clay.

- The crow and his actions are the focus of this story. Ask questions that will encourage the children to explore the story in greater depth, e.g. ask about the crow's general appearance, actions, way of thinking, role in this particular story, etc. Scribe the children's ideas on a chart. Add illustrations.

- Make pictures of crows using a variety of collage materials. Remind the children to look closely at the illustrations in their books.

Using the blackline master

- Read the words in the boxes. Demonstrate 'cloze procedure'. Remind the children to check the text for meaning.

My name is _____

_____

| stones | clever | flew |
| crow | tree | drink |

It was a very hot day.

A big black bird called a crow
wanted to have a _____ of water.

He looked down from a _____.

He saw a pot and _____ down
to have a good look at it.

The _____ was a big bird.

His head was too big to get inside the pot.

So he put some _____ into the pot.

The water came up inside the pot, little by little.

Then the _____ crow had a drink of water.

Blackline master 14 • *The Crow and the Pot* © Nelson, 2000.

This page may be photocopied for educational use within the purchasing institution.

PM Plus Teachers' Guide: Levels 12–14   61

New Glasses for Max

About the story
Children who have been laughed at while wearing glasses, will understand Max's reluctance to wear his new glasses. This text provides an opportunity to explore a text layout that emphasises dialogue cues.

Linking with other PM books
Max and Grandad series   PM Plus Levels 6–11
The Optometrist   PM Library N. F. Blue Level
A Friend for Max   PM Plus Level 12
Max and Jake   PM Plus Level 12

Creating the atmosphere
Read *The Optometrist* with the children. Explain that an optometrist tests people's eyes to see if they need glasses. Encourage those children who have been to an optometrist to discuss their experiences and the procedures involved.

Focusing on the story
- **Cover** Recall other stories about Max and Grandad. Read the title. Discuss how important it is to be able to see clearly.

- **Pages 2–7** Discuss with the children who they should tell if they 'can't see the words'.

- **Pages 8–9** Talk about Max's revealing statement. Ask the children to compare it with their own experiences.

- **Pages 10–13** Max is very proud of his dad! Discuss the coping strategies that Grandad gives to Max. Ask, 'How do you think Max will feel about wearing glasses now?' Observe the text layout with space separating the dialogue between speakers.

- **Pages 14–16** Confirm Max's friendship with Jake. Check the illustrations for the likeness between Max and his dad.

Going beyond the story
- Discuss how to effectively care for your eyes. Make a poster or booklet.

- Reread *My Little Sister* (PM Library Non-fiction Blue Level). Discuss the physical similarities between the two girls. Invite the children to describe and then draw pictures of family members who look alike. Encourage the children to write descriptive captions.

- Role-play positive and negative things that happen during play and classroom situations. Discuss words, voice tone, actions and body language.

Developing specific skills
- Revisit changing the final consonant: ha*s*, ha*d*; hi*s*, hi*d*.
- Revisit *ph* (PM Library Alphabet Blends book).
- Discuss possessive apostrophes: Max's eyes.
- Discuss the plural form of 'glasses'.

Using the blackline master
- Read the sentences with the children. Ask them to choose the word that retains the meaning.
- Discuss the qualities of a friend. Write the children's ideas on a chart. Have them refer to these ideas as they complete the blackline master.

My name is _____

do	does	don't

Max looked in the mirror.

"I _____ look like my dad," he said.

"I _____ care if that boy laughs at me.

Jake is my best friend
and he _____ not laugh at me."

___

My best friend is

_____.

We _____

_____

_____

_____

Lollipop, the Old Car

About the story
This story, involving some animated vehicles, suggests that 'slow and steady wins the race'. Imaginary narrative texts give the reader opportunities to explain how the personalities of the characters affect the plot.

Linking with other PM books
The Toytown Helicopter	PM Plus Level 5
The Toytown Fire Engine	PM Plus level 6
The Fire on Toytown Hill	PM Plus Level 9
The Toytown Racing Car	PM Plus level 11

Creating the atmosphere
Read *The Hare and the Tortoise* (PM Library Traditional Tales and Plays Purple Level). Discuss the events in the story.

Focusing on the story
- **Cover** Read the title. Explain that the animated vehicles in this story have personalities and are able to talk.
- **Pages 2–7** Talk about the different facial expressions and what these tell the reader about the vehicles' personalities. Predict what might happen next. Ask the children to check their predictions as they read the story.
- **Pages 8–9** The flag is down; the race begins!
- **Pages 10–11** Discuss the red racing car's attitude. Compare this attitude with the hare's in *The Hare and the Tortoise*.
- **Pages 12–13** Talk about the illustrations before reading the text. Notice that the front entrance to the park can be seen at the top of the hill.
- **Pages 14–16** Discuss the satisfying ending.

Going beyond the story
- Draw a mural of the racetrack. Have the children draw, cut out and then paste the vehicles onto the mural. Invite the children to write stories about the events. Paste these onto the mural.
- Using card, make stand-up models of the vehicles. Draw their facial expressions. Write descriptive captions to place beside the models.

This is the red racing car. It thinks it will win the race because it goes fast. Ling

- Make a board game that involves a race. Help the children to draw the track on a long piece of card. Mark 20 even spaces and number each. On some of the spaces write 'Miss a turn' and a reason why (ensure it links with the story), e.g. 'went to sleep'. Use little plastic cars as counters. Roll a die for each turn.

Developing specific skills
- Search the text for two adjectives before a verb: *little blue* cars, *big green* car, etc.
- Compare the meanings: won, one.
- Revisit consonant blends: *slowly, sleep, start, smiled.* Recall other words that begin the same way.

Using the blackline master
- Revisit page 16 of the story. Have the children complete the illustration and the text.
- Encourage the children to revisit the text for information to help them with their writing.

My name is _____

Lollipop, _____ _____, _____ _____,

_____ _____ _____ _____.

The little blue cars did not win.

They _____.

The big green car did not win.

It _____.

The red racing car did not win.

It _____.

Locked In

About the story
Dad puts a lock on the door of the budgies' cage so no one can take the budgies away. The humorous context of this story is supported by detailed illustrations to help young readers access meaning effectively.

Linking with other PM books

Locked Out	PM Library Blue Level
Pete Little	PM Library Green Level
The Lost Keys	PM Plus Level 12
Budgies	PM Library N. F. Orange Level

Creating the atmosphere

Read *Budgies* to the children. Discuss how to care for budgies. Encourage the children to talk about their own experiences.

Focusing on the story

- **Cover** Introduce the new characters. The budgies are family pets. Observe the walk-in aviary with a large outer door. Explain that budgies cannot live without a built shelter in cold climates.

- **Pages 2–3** Discuss how Adam and his family provide quality care for their budgies.

- **Pages 4–5** Talk about the purpose of locks. Point out that keys are now required to open the cage.

- **Pages 6–9** Notice that Dad has his hands full and that the keys are still in the lock. Have the children read to find out how the door shut. Recall why Dad cannot open the door!

- **Pages 10–13** Read these pages with expression.

- **Pages 14–16** Discuss the humorous ending.

Going beyond the story

- Talk about what happened at the beginning, the middle and the end of the story. Provide the children with long strips of paper and have them fold these into three. Ask the children to write about the story, sequencing the events into three parts.

- Discuss the detailed illustrations in the story. Provide pastels or small crayons for the children to make pictures of their favourite illustrations. Display the pictures with appropriate captions.

- Recall the climax of the story. Talk about funny situations that the children have experienced. Have them write and draw about these. Collect the stories and make them into a concertina booklet.

> *Funny stories*
> • One day Jana was walking under an apple tree when an apple fell on her head.

Developing specific skills
- Revise recognition of colour names.
- Discuss 'ck' ending: back, stuck, lock.
- Revise intonation as an expression of meaning. Practise examples from the text.
- Compare the meanings: blew, blue.

Using the blackline master
- Read pages 2–3 of the text. Read the sentence clue for number one across.
- Show the children how to record the first word on the crossword. Read the other sentences together.
- Have the children complete the crossword.

My name is _____

Across

1. Adam and his mum and dad loved _____.

3. The budgies were in a big cage
   in the back _____.

5. One day Dad left
   the key in the lock
   on the _____
   of the cage.

6. Now Dad was locked
   _____ the cage.

Down

2. "Help!" cried Dad.
   "The _____ will not open."

4. Adam came home from school.
   He _____ to look for Dad.

5. "Please _____ the door and let me out,"
   said Dad.

7. "You _____ look funny, Dad," said Adam.

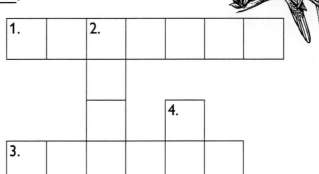

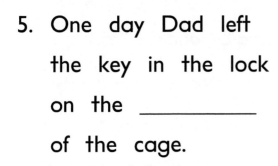

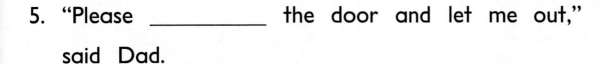

Popcorn Fun

About the story

Many children will have made popcorn. This experience will allow them to recognise the theme of the story and relate naturally to the visual language in the text, e.g. 'The popcorn went round and round inside.'

Linking with other PM books

Roar Like a Tiger	PM Plus Level 8
Katie's Caterpillar	PM Plus Level 8
Joe Makes a House	PM Plus Level 10
The Broken Flower Pot	PM Plus Level 11

Creating the atmosphere

Make some popcorn. If possible, use a popcorn maker. Observe how the popcorn changes colour and shape. Encourage the children to talk about the smell of the popcorn as it cooks and the sound it makes.

Focusing on the story

- **Cover** Read the title and discuss the cover illustration.

- **Pages 2–5** Compare Mum's idea for a wet-day activity with activities that the children do at home on wet days. Explain that popcorn balls are made by rolling the popcorn in liquid honey.

- **Pages 6–9** Ensure that the children understand how the popcorn maker works. Recall that the popcorn will be hot when it spills out of the spout.

- **Pages 10–11** Predict what might happen while Mum is away.

- **Pages 12–16** Check the children's predictions. Discuss Mum's laughing response to Katie and Joe's mischievous actions.

Going beyond the story

- Discuss times when the children have eaten popcorn. Write and draw about these occasions.

- Popcorn has a very distinctive smell as it is cooking. Ask the children to name other cooking smells they like. List their ideas. Have them write about their favourite cooking smells. Gather the children's stories and make them into a book entitled 'Our Favourite Cooking Smells'.

> Sometimes we have pancakes for breakfast. Yum! / We put maple syrup on them.

- If left unsweetened, popcorn is a healthy snack. Discuss other healthy snacks and the reasons why they are healthy. Invite the children to make posters about healthy snacks.

- Make some popcorn in a popcorn maker. Help the children to list the procedures involved.

Developing specific skills

- Discuss words ending in 'y': sticky, ready, honey.
- Revisit contractions: it's, won't, let's, don't.
- Talk about opposites: up, down; hot, cold; long, short; in, out.
- Discover base words: make, maker; stick, sticky.

Using the blackline master

- Read the words in the first box. Talk about which one is better. Complete the first sentence together.
- Explain what opposites are. Have the children search their texts for the other words.
- Talk about what they will draw in their pictures.

My name is _____

Katie and Joe _____ some popcorn.

make	made

The popcorn _____ out of the popcorn maker.

come	came

It _____ into the bowl on the table.

fall	fell

Katie _____ some of the hot popcorn.

take	took

It was too hot. She _____ on it.

blow	blew

Write the opposites.

up	down		white	black
in	_____		inside	_____
cold	_____		on	_____

Coco's Bell

About the story

Rosie becomes distressed when a sparrow dies after Coco, her cat, traps it with his paws. Being aware that cats are meat eaters and hunters makes the meaning easier to understand.

Linking with other PM books

Pussy and the birds	PM Library Red Level
Brown Mouse series	PM Plus Levels 8–10
Max and the Bird House	PM Plus Level 11
The Picnic Boat	PM Plus Level 12

Creating the atmosphere

Reread *Pussy and the Birds*. Invite the children to talk about their own negative experiences with cats. Explain that cats are meat eaters (carnivorous).

Focusing on the story

- **Cover** Read the title together. Talk about why a cat might wear a bell.

- **Pages 2–3** Discuss the illustration before reading the text. Examine Rosie's expression. How is she feeling?

- **Pages 4–7** Read these pages with expression. Talk about what Rosie could do to care for the hurt bird.

- **Pages 8–11** Observe how gently Rosie and her dad care for the injured bird.

- **Pages 12–13** Allow the children time to talk about the dead bird. Recall why cats need to spend time outdoors.

- **Pages 14–16** Have the children search the text for Dad's solution to the problem. Discuss other occasions when a bell 'rings a warning'.

Developing specific skills

- Revise the pronouns: he, him; she, her.
- Observe irregular verb forms: ring, rang; fly, flew.
- Recall other words that begin with: *br* — *broken*, *st* — *stayed*, *gr* — *grass*.
- Discuss the sound 'ow' makes in: window, showed.

Going beyond the story

- Discuss the 'naughty' things that cats sometimes do. Make a list of the children's ideas. Have them write about their ideas. Paste the writing onto large cards to form a concertina floor story.

- Reread a selection of PM Plus and PM Library books that feature cats (see 'Linking with other PM books'). Invite the children to rewrite their favourite stories in their own words.

- Talk about the reason for Coco's bell, i.e. it is a warning device. Make a poster about other warning devices.

- Have the children make pencil sketches of a cat about to pounce on its unsuspecting prey. Use descriptive vocabulary, e.g. 'legs bent', 'crouching low', etc. to describe the cat's actions.

Using the blackline master

- Have the children retell the procedures Rosie and Dad followed. Revisit the text if necessary.
- Read through the 'helpful words'. Encourage the children to use these in their writing. Add an appropriate illustration.
- Complete the second section following the same procedure.

My name is _____

Rosie and Dad looked after the bird.

They _____

_____

_____

_____

Helpful words

box   towel   food   water   morning

Rosie and dad went to the shops.

They _____

_____

_____

_____

Helpful words

bell   runs   away   ring   fly

The Classroom Caterpillars

About the story

A problem arises when Katie, and her friend Anna, find some very hungry caterpillars have eaten all the swan plant leaves. Problem solving helps young readers think critically about how meaning is conveyed.

Linking with other PM books

Katie's Caterpillar	PM Plus Level 8
Making a Caterpillar	PM Plus N. F. Levels 8 & 9
Walking in the Summer	PM Library N. F. Green Level

Creating the atmosphere

Bring a swan plant (milkweed) into the classroom and talk about the monarch butterfly's life cycle. Discuss photographs that show the four stages of the cycle.

Focusing on the story

- **Cover** Read the title and discuss the cover illustration. Identify Katie from previous PM Plus stories.

- **Pages 2–3** Talk about the illustration before reading the text. Discuss the need to care for living things.

- **Pages 4–5** Talk about the beginning of the life cycle. Observe the tiny white eggs under the leaf.

- **Pages 6–11** Notice how Katie's caterpillar is much bigger than the others. Observe how their sizes change and the swan plant becomes bare! Are the children able to offer Katie solutions?

- **Pages 12–16** Discuss the meaning of the word 'chrysalis'. Talk about the satisfactory ending to the story and the anticipated completion of the life cycle.

Going beyond the story

- Discuss how the text confirms the three stages of the monarch butterfly's life cycle. Discuss the fourth stage together. Show the children how to record the stages on strips of paper folded into four.

- Bring a swan plant (milkweed) into the classroom. Ensure that monarch butterflies have laid eggs on the leaves. Watch the hungry caterpillars grow bigger and bigger! Count the number of days it takes for a chrysalis to turn into a butterfly. Observe how the butterflies dry their wings before flying away.

- Study photographs of butterflies. Identify the symmetrical designs. Have the children draw butterflies with symmetrical designs on their wings.

- Grow some swan plant seeds in containers and observe their development.

Developing specific skills

- Revise the names for days of the week.
- Encourage self-monitoring by using the illustrations to check meaning.
- Discuss the plural: leaf, leaves.

Using the blackline master

- Discuss the life cycle of a butterfly.
- Demonstrate how the children will draw and write about the cycle.
- Complete the first sentence together.

My name is _____
_____

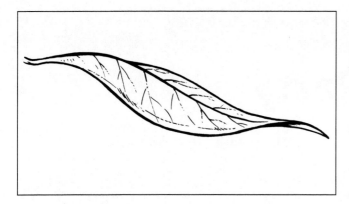

First_____

_____

_____

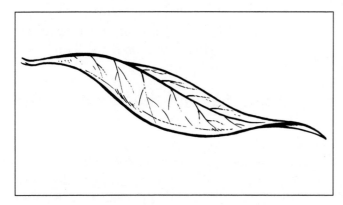

Then _____

_____

_____

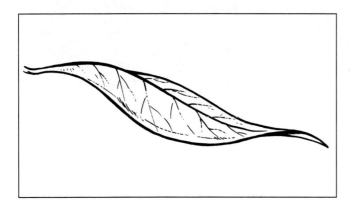

After that_____

_____

_____

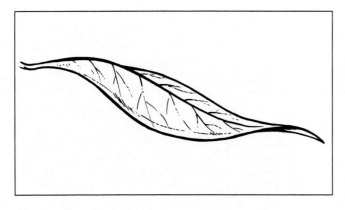

One day it will _____

_____

_____

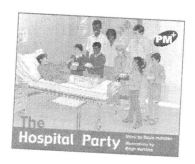

The Hospital Party

About the story

Many children will sympathise with Adam when he is unable to attend his friend's birthday party. The context of this story encourages readers to predict, check and confirm until a very satisfactory ending becomes evident.

Linking with other PM books

Birthday balloons	PM Library Blue Level
Birthday Presents	PM Plus Level 11
The babysitter	PM Library Green Level
Locked In	PM Plus Level 13

Creating the atmosphere

Reread *My accident* (PM Library Starters Two). Invite the children who have had accidents and been admitted to a hospital ward to talk about their experiences.

Focusing on the story

- **Cover** Read the title together and discuss the cover illustration. Inform the children that a broken leg requires a short stay in hospital.

- **Page 2–3** Talk about why Adam is unhappy. Invite the children to share reasons why they have sometimes been unable to attend special events.

- **Pages 4–7** Discuss activities that keep children occupied while in bed. Talk about the responsibilities of nurses towards their patients.

- **Pages 8–9** Encourage the children to suggest what might happen next.

- **Pages 10–11** Read to confirm the children's predictions.

- **Pages 12–16** Compare the different forms of greetings used by friends. Invite

the children to comment on the special friendship between Adam and Tim.

Going beyond the story

- Talk about times when the children have been unable to attend special events. Invite them to write about their experiences. Ask them to check that their stories tell: what, when and why. Bind the stories together to make a book.

> On the day that my class was going to Waterworld, I woke up with a sore throat.
>
> Mum said that I had to stay in bed.
>
> Sanson

- Have the children list activities that they might enjoy if they were confined to bed. Invite them to read their lists aloud. Identify those activities that are more popular than others.

- Invite the children to design and make birthday cards for friends or family members.

Developing specific skills

- Revise compound words: birth/day, pop/corn, to/day.
- Find the base word: broke — broken.
- Clap the syllables: hos/pi/tal, child/ren, bro/ken, par/ty.
- Recognise the sound 'ar' in: card, party.

Using the blackline master

- Revisit regular plurals. Have the children write the plurals and draw matching pictures.
- Identify compound words. List some on a chart.
- Read the sentences together. Invite the children to draw matching pictures. Check the text for details.

My name is _____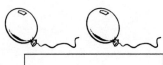

one balloon    **two** balloons

one friend   two_____

one pen    two_____

today   to   day

birthday   birth   _____

popcorn   _____   _____

himself   _____   _____

Adam did not want to stay in hospital.	Adam smiled. "I like hospital parties," he said.

Swimming with a Dragon

About the story
In this story, the teacher includes the class in an innovative way to help one of the children overcome a fear of water. 'Reading the illustrations' will help children read the text with understanding and expression.

Linking with other PM books
Little Chimp and the Bees	PM Plus Level 9
Come on, Tim	PM Library Blue Level
Max and Jake	PM Plus Level 12
Sam's Haircut	PM Plus Level 13

Creating the atmosphere
Talk about why people (not just children) often feel nervous when learning something new. Discuss forms of encouragement that might help these people

Focusing on the story
- **Cover** Study the illustration and read the title. Predict what might happen in the story.
- **Pages 2–3** Observe Yasmin's facial expressions and body language.
- **Pages 4–5** Yasmin's nervousness is obvious. Notice how she looks downwards. Her friends offer encouragement but she is unable to venture further into the water.
- **Pages 6–7** Talk about how the balloons will be made into a dragon.
- **Pages 8–11** Discuss why the inflated balloons will float. Observe how Yasmin joins in.
- **Pages 12–13** Discuss the illustration before reading the text. Ask, 'Why is Yasmin climbing down the ladder slowly?'

Developing specific skills
- Recall other words that begin like 'across': about.
- Discuss 'there' and 'their'. Demonstrate when they are used.
- Revise words ending in 'ly': slow*ly*.

- **Pages 14–16** Talk about forms of encouragement. Discuss how it feels when something difficult is accomplished.

Going beyond the story
- Have the children bring photos of themselves learning or achieving something new. Encourage them to talk and write about their photos.
- Distinguish between different feelings, e.g. feeling happy, sad, nervous, etc. List the children's ideas on a chart. Have them write about their ideas. Collate the stories and make a book entitled 'Feelings'.

I always feel happy when I go to stay with Nana. She spoils me. She reads me lots of stories.

- Ask the children to make dragons from green, yellow and red balloons. Have them refer to the illustrations in the story. Remind them to add eyes, nostrils, scales, etc.

Using the blackline master
- Study the illustrations on the blackline master closely. Ensure that the children are able to explain the sequence of events.
- Complete the first sentence together. Have the children complete the remainder of the blackline master independently.

My name is _____
_____

1. First _____

_____

_____ .

2. Then _____

_____

_____ .

3. After that_____

_____

_____ .

4. At last _____

_____

_____ .

The Wheelbarrow Garden

About the story

This story is a sequel to *Look in the Garden*. Both books reflect the non-fiction theme of food and eating. The frequent repetition of familiar, heavy-duty words encourages confident reading.

Linking with other PM books

Sally's beans	PM Library Yellow Level
Look in the Garden	PM Plus Level 12
Making a Caterpillar	PM Plus N. F. Levels 8 & 9

Creating the atmosphere

Soak some pea seeds overnight. Plant them in a flower pot or miniature terrarium made from the lower half of a plastic drink bottle. Check that the container has drainage holes, before adding stones, sand and potting mix.

Focusing on the story

- **Cover** Read the title together. Ask the children what they think the boys are doing. Explain that this story is a sequel to *Look in the Garden*.

- **Pages 2–3** Study the illustration. Discuss the meaning of the word 'room', i.e. space.

- **Pages 4–7** Discuss alternative garden choices, e.g. flower pots, window boxes, etc. for gardens where space is limited.

- **Pages 8–11** Ensure that the children check meaning by confirming that visual and meaning clues match. Talk about why the wheelbarrow is placed in the sun, and why sand and pebbles, as well as potting mix, are needed.

- **Pages 12–16** Discuss the support and advice offered by the parents. Observe the boys' shared sense of pride and satisfaction.

Going beyond the story

- Arrange for the children to visit a local nursery or garden centre. Or, invite a horticulturist into the class to demonstrate growing and caring for plants.

- Grow alfalfa, mustard or cress seeds. Place a spoonful of seeds into a plastic jar. Cover them with warm water and leave the seeds to soak for approximately five minutes. Place a muslin or old stocking cover over the top of the jar. Tip the jar onto its side so that the water runs out. Repeat this procedure twice daily. Keep the jar in a warm place. Within several days, the seed sprouts may be eaten in a salad or sandwich.

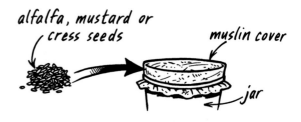

alfalfa, mustard or cress seeds — muslin cover — jar

Developing specific skills

- Revise the possessive apostrophe: Scott's house, Scott's place, Scott's dad, Scott's mother.
- Confirm quick recognition of high-frequency words.
- Revise punctuation: question and exclamation marks.

Using the blackline master

- Study the illustrations. Have the children recall the procedures James and Scott followed.
- Discuss how the children will write the instructions.
- Read the instructions for section two with the children.

My name is _____

How to make a wheelbarrow garden

- Put _____

  _____

- Put _____

  _____

- Plant _____

  _____

- Water _____

  _____

Turn this page over.

Draw a picture of the wheelbarrow garden.

Teasing Mum

About the story
This is another story about the twins, Matthew and Emma. Mum and the twins have lots of fun playing on a hot summer's day. The familiar context encourages children to relate their own personal experiences.

Linking with other PM books
Brown Mouse Plays a Trick	PM Plus Level 9
The Beach House	PM Plus Level 9
Rabbits' Ears	PM Plus level 10
Teasing Dad	PM Library Blue Level

Creating the atmosphere
Demonstrate how to fix a hose onto a tap. Help the children discover how the water flow from the hose can be adjusted by turning the tap.

Focusing on the story
- **Cover** Read the title together. Discuss the meaning of the word 'teasing'. Study the illustration. Predict what might happen in the story.
- **Pages 2–5** Talk about ideal growing conditions for plants. Discuss alternative watering systems during dry times. Ask, 'How are the children helping?'
- **Pages 6–7** Discuss the illustration before reading the text. Predict why the water flow has stopped.
- **Pages 8–11** Discuss Matthew's mischievous trick! Ensure that the children understand what happened once Matthew lifted his foot off the hose.
- **Pages 12–16** Talk about how Mum and Emma showed that they understood Matthew's teasing.

Going beyond the story
- Talk about where water comes from, what happens to it, how it is used, etc. Write a summary on the whiteboard. Have the children write about and draw their ideas. Bind their work together to make a book entitled 'What We Know About Water'.
- Revisit other PM Plus stories about Matthew and Emma from Levels 3–10. Have the children take notes on the things they know about each member of the family. Discuss their ideas. Assist the children to write simple character studies.

> Matthew is Emma's twin brother. They share the same birthday. Matthew likes to tease. He makes his mum laugh.

- Invite the children to write and draw about teasing experiences they have been involved in.
- Discuss what plants need in order to grow. Record the children's ideas on a chart. Have them add matching illustrations.

Developing specific skills
- Revise contractions: it's, that's, can't, I'm.
- Find words that begin like: *trick, stuck, slowly*.
- Revise verb endings: turn, turned; fix, fixed.
- Find other words that end like 'water' and 'better'.

Using the blackline master
- Read the words in the shaded boxes. Discuss the similar verb endings. Have the children discuss which word 'makes sense'.
- Invite the children to draw Matthew trying to run past Mum.

My name is _____

watered	turned	moved
tried	played	stopped

Matthew fixed the hose onto the tap and _____ it on.

Mum _____ the garden with the hose.

But the hose got stuck under a rock.

Emma _____ it away.

Then Matthew put his foot down on the hose and the water _____.

He _____ a trick on Mum.

She ran after Matthew.

He _____ to run past her.

Turn this page over.

Draw a picture of Matthew trying to run past Mum.

Katie's Butterfly

About the story

This scientifically accurate narrative completes the life cycle of Katie's caterpillar. Anxiety will keep children turning the pages until Katie's ingenuity provides a platform for the butterfly's first fluttering flight.

Linking with other PM books

Katie's Caterpillar	PM Plus Level 8
The Classroom Caterpillars	PM Plus Level 13
Walking in the Summer	PM Library N. F. Green Level

Creating the atmosphere

Reread *The Classroom Caterpillars*. Review the four stages of development in the monarch butterfly's life cycle.

Focusing on the story

- **Cover** Read the title together. Explain that this story is a sequel to *The Classroom Caterpillars*.

- **Pages 2–5** Observe how the butterfly holds onto the chrysalis case. Explain that the two front legs are very small and do not function as such. Tell the children that the butterfly's wings require at least an hour to elapse before they become dry and firm.

- **Pages 6–9** Explain that the butterfly has special claws at the end of its walking legs for hanging onto vegetation. Talk about how these would cling to the fibre in Katie's woollen cardigan.

- **Pages 10–16** Compare the aero-dynamics of the butterfly with that of launching a kite.

Going beyond the story

- Read stories about butterflies to the children, e.g. *The Very Hungry Caterpillar* by Eric Carle (Hamish Hamilton, 1970).

- Provide the children with butterfly-shaped pieces of paper. Have them drop spoonfuls of different coloured paint onto one half of the paper. Invite the children to then fold the other half on top, and press firmly. When opened out, symmetrical patterns will appear.

- Cut butterfly shapes from folded pieces of firm paper. Colour the butterflies brightly before making them into butterfly kites. Tie a piece of string just below the centre of one front wing to the centre of the other. Then tie a long piece of string to just below the middle of this first piece of string. When the kites catch the breeze, the wings curve and the breeze below lifts them into the air.

Using the blackline master

- Have the children revisit the text and search for details in the illustrations.
- List information about Katie's butterfly on a chart. Have the children refer to this as they write.
- Discuss other information about butterflies the children might like to record.

Developing specific skills

- Clap the syllables in: but/ter/fly, beau/ti/ful, chry/sa/lis.
- Revise irregular verbs: fly, flew; run, ran; fall, fell.
- Use punctuation to aid reading with expression.

My name is _____

Draw a picture about Katie's butterfly.

Katie's butterfly _____

_____

_____

_____

_____

_____

The Nest on the Beach

About the story

The accurately presented setting of this narrative gives reason for the agitation experienced by a sea bird when its nesting environment is threatened. Understanding the effect of setting is an essential feature of narrative texts.

Linking with other PM books

Baby Hippo	PM Library Yellow Level
A Treasure Island	PM Plus Level 11
Down by the Sea	PM Plus Level 11
The Jungle Frogs	PM Plus Level 12

Creating the atmosphere

Show pictures of oyster catcher sea birds which belong to the pied stilt family. The nesting habits described in this text are common for members of this family.

Focusing on the story

- **Cover** Read the title and discuss the illustration. Identify Meg and Gran from previous PM Plus stories.
- Talk about:
— why the bird thought Meg and Gran were a threat
— what body language signals were given by the bird
— how the bird tried to draw Meg and Gran away from the nesting area
— how the colour of the eggs helped to camouflage them
— why the barrier was protective, i.e. wide enough out from the nest not to intimidate the bird
— how the children could protect bird life in their own community.

Developing specific skills

- Revise possessive apostrophes: bird's nest.
- List words that rhyme with: dry, sand, back, beach, nest, still. Discuss the letter clusters common to each list of words.
- Revise other adverbs that begin like 'across'.

Going beyond the story

- Discuss the sequence of events featured in the story. List them on a chart. Have the children write about and draw these. Display the writing as a wall story. Encourage the children to record the dialogue in speech bubbles.
- Talk about how the children could contribute to protecting birds and wild-life in their environment. Write their ideas on a poster and invite them to add illustrations.
- Talk about the actions taken by different animals to protect their young.

> A mother crocodile can put her babies inside her mouth and keep them there until it is safe for them to come out.
> Liam

- Discuss the body language of the sea bird. Look closely at the illustrations of it in the book. Ask the children to complete a pencil drawing of the bird.

Using the blackline master

- Discuss the illustrations the children will draw in the boxes.
- Demonstrate how to search the text to find pages referred to in the blackline master.

My name is _____
_____

The bird ran across the sand.

It _____

_____

The bird ran back down the beach.

It _____

_____

But the bird was not happy.

It _____

_____

The bird was happy now.

It _____

_____

The Fawn in the Forest

About the story
Reading this narrative aloud will enhance children's awareness of the literary phrases and rhythms of language. The illustrations and information in the story capture the true behaviour of many species of deer.

Linking with other PM books
The Swan Family	PM Plus Level 10
Little Chimp and Baby Chimp	PM Plus Level 10
Mother Tiger and her Cubs	PM Plus Level 11
The Jungle Frogs	PM Plus Level 12

Creating the atmosphere
Show the children pictures of animals that protect themselves by using camouflage. Alternatively, read *Look at Colour and Camouflage* by Rachel Wright (Franklin Watts, 1989) to the children.

Focusing on the story
- **Cover** Read the title. Discuss the cover and title page illustrations.
- **Pages 2–3** Discuss the rhythmic pattern of the text. Explain that the spots on the fawn's coat help it to hide from its enemies. The spots gradually disappear when a fawn is about six weeks old.
- **Pages 4–5** Discuss the concept of camouflage in relation to the phrase 'spots of sunlight on the leaves'.
- **Pages 6–13** Observe how the forest scene doesn't appear in its entirety but rather 'pans' across the landscape.
- **Pages 14–16** Discuss the story's conclusion. It is recommended that the teacher read the book aloud, reinforcing the rhythms and sentence structures before the children read the text again.

Going beyond the story
- Have the children draw pictures of animals camouflaged against their natural backgrounds. Paste these into a scrapbook. Ask the children to write about their pictures. The 'camouflage scrapbook' can be added to at other times.
- Invite the children to make clay models of animals that have colours to match their surroundings. Have them then draw appropriate landscapes for their models to be displayed against.
- Make a mask for each of the characters in the story. Invite children to wear these as they mime the actions of the characters. Another child can read the story aloud as the drama unfolds.
- Encourage the children to write a piece of poetic writing, recreating the rhythmic structure of the text.

Trees
Shady trees,
Leaves on the ground.
Spots of sunlight on the leaves,
Shadows all around.
A secret place.

Developing specific skills
- Discuss the verbs: lay, laying; try, tried; hide, hiding.
- Find base words, e.g. 'hidden' from 'hide'.
- Revisit pronouns: he, his, her, him, himself.
- Revise blends: *place, play; stayed, still; grass, green.*

Using the blackline master
- Have the children retell the story.
- Read the blackline master together. Show the children how to search the text for the missing words.
- Invite the children to add their own illustrations.

My name is _____

_____

A baby fawn lay hiding in the
green _____.

He lay in the leaves in the long
grass under the _____.

He lay in a secret _____.

He did not move his _____.

He did not move his _____.

He stayed very still.

He did not move his _____.

He did not move his _____.

He did not try to find his mother.

He was safe if he stayed _____.

The Skipping Rope

About the story
Children who can skip, as well as children who can't, will relate personally with the context of this story. Reading becomes personal and meaningful when the reader relates the characters' experiences with their own.

Linking with other PM books

Sam Plays Swing Ball	PM Plus Level 9
Sam's Painting	PM Plus Level 10
Come on, Tim	PM Library Blue Level
Try again, Hannah	PM Library Green Level

Creating the atmosphere
Provide the children with an opportunity to show their skipping prowess. Talk about the actions required to keep the rope moving while it is being jumped over.

Focusing on the story
- **Cover** Introduce the new characters — Abby and Clare. Read the title and discuss the illustration.
- **Pages 3–16** Link the illustrations to the children's own experiences. Draw their attention to:
— Abby's despondency when she saw Clare's skipping prowess
— Clare's encouragement
— Clare's instructions to Abby
— Abby's concentration as she tries to master a new skill
— Clare's perception that a shorter rope would be more suitable for Abby
— Abby's growing confidence as she begins to skip properly
— Abby's effort, persevering until she was finally successful.

Developing specific skills
- Discuss compound words: outside, without.
- Read noting intonation signs: bold print, exclamation marks (helps to express the author's intention).
- Find words that begin with: tr, st, sk.

Encourage the children to reinforce their understandings by linking these ideas with their own experiences.

Going beyond the story
- Play skipping games, e.g. teach the actions to 'Teddy Bear, Teddy Bear'.
- Talk about new skills the children have mastered at home or at school. Discuss the perseverance that is often required when learning a new skill. Scribe the children's ideas on a chart. Follow up the discussion with writing and drawing.

> I kept falling off my bike.
> I got back on again.
> I kept on trying.
> Now I can ride it
> without wobbling around.   Daniel

- Talk about giving instructions. Reread page 4 to identify what Clare said to help Abby learn to skip. With the children, write instructions for something they will be able to do independently, e.g. how to make a sandwich.

Using the blackline master
- Read the words in the boxes. Talk about the similarities and differences between them.
- Complete the first two sentences together.
- Discuss the pattern the children will follow when making new words.

My name is ________________________________

Abby always ____________ going to play with her friend Clare.

liked lived

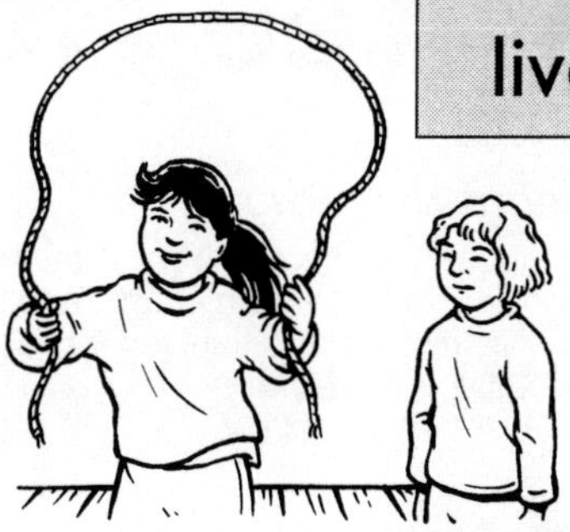

Clare ____________ on a farm.

One day, Clare said, "Let's skip!"

Abby ____________ to skip.

But she ____________ over the rope.

tried tripped

Abby turned the rope.

She let it ____________ on the ground, and then she jumped over the rope.

still stay

"I'm ____________ not very good at it," said Abby. "I want to skip like you."

Make new words. Read them to a friend.

look	looks	looking	looked
stay	stays	________	________
turn	________	________	________

A Tree Horse

About the story
In this story, Clare and Abby pretend that a tree branch is a horse. There are many purposeful opportunities for talking, reading and thinking while students recreate meaning from this story.

Linking with other PM books
The Leaf Boats	PM Plus Level 7
A Crocodile and a Whale	PM Plus Level 7
Joe Makes a House	PM Plus Level 10
Tom's Ride	PM Plus Level 11

Creating the atmosphere
Reread *A Crocodile and a Whale*. Encourage the children to talk about their own imaginative play experiences.

Focusing on the story
- **Cover** Explain that the setting and characters are the same as in *The Skipping Rope*. Read the title. Predict what the story might be about.

- **Pages 2–5** Read these pages to find out what the girls did because of their shared interest in horses.

- **Pages 6–9** Study the illustrations. Notice that the low branch is safe for the girls to scramble up onto. Discuss rules for safe play.

- **Pages 10–16** Encourage the children to talk and think about the illustrations as they read the text, e.g. the towel draped over the branch resembles a saddle, the rope is the bridle, etc. Some children could mime the girls' actions as they made their horse go 'faster'.

Going beyond the story
- Provide the children with a selection of books, photographs, newspaper articles and videos about horses to extend their understandings. Have them record information or share it orally.

- Talk about the children's own imaginative play experiences. Record their ideas on the whiteboard. Have them write about and draw their ideas. Display the children's work as a concertina booklet.

- In pairs, have the children role-play the story from page 6 onwards. Ask them to include dialogue between the two girls, as in the book.

- Make posters about 'Safe Play'.

Developing specific skills
- Revise verb endings: ed — lov*ed*, paint*ed*, want*ed*, liv*ed*, climb*ed*; ing — mov*ing*, rid*ing*, go*ing*.
- Discuss rhyming words and add new words: get, met, __; down, town, __; mat, cat, __; for, door, __.
- Discuss the possessive pronoun 'their'.

Using the blackline master
- Discuss the first picture. Write the children's explanation of what is happening on the whiteboard so that it can be used as a model.
- Discuss the other pictures and have some children share what they will write.

My name is _____

Write about each picture.

_____

_____

_____

_____

_____

_____

_____

_____

_____

Red Squirrel's Adventure

About the story
This narrative (without dialogue) is a factual story based upon a true incident between three characters: a red squirrel, a goshawk and an eagle. Every page has clues that lead dramatically to the events on the next page.

Linking with other PM books
The Little White Hen	PM Plus Level 8
Baby Hippo	PM Library Yellow Level
Mother Tiger and her Cubs	PM Plus Level 11
Three Little Mice in Trouble	PM Plus Level 13

Creating the atmosphere
Reread *Red Squirrel Hides Some Nuts* (PM Plus Level 7). On a chart, list all the information that children know about squirrels.

Focusing on the story
- **Cover** Read the title together and discuss the illustration.

- **Pages 2–3** Ensure that the children understand that Red Squirrel will be vulnerable when she goes to get the nut.

- **Pages 4–9** Draw the children's attention to the goshawk swooping towards the squirrel, feet thrust out and large claws ready to grab!

- **Pages 10–13** Identify the aggressive eagle, with its large wing-span, as another predator. Discuss each bird's unique colours and fighting attributes.

- **Pages 14–16** Discuss Red Squirrels' lucky escape. Talk about her agility in the treetops and how quickly she seeks a safe retreat. Discuss other animals that live in fear of being prey for larger animals.

Going beyond the story
- Review the events of the story in sequential order. Have the children rewrite the story as if they were Red Squirrel. Begin the first sentence together, e.g. 'One day I was eating a nut when suddenly ...'

- Write facts about squirrels on squirrel-shaped paper.

- Make a mural of the forest from collage materials. Have the children make cardboard cut-outs of the three characters. Put Blu-Tack on the back of each cut-out. Ask the children to move the characters as they retell the story.

- Discuss how some small animals have developed behaviours to avoid being easy prey for larger animals. Discuss the use of camouflage and physical deterrents, e.g prickles, smells, burrows, etc. Make a wall story about these behaviours.

Developing specific skills
- Read *sk, squ, fl, gr* (PM Library Alphabet Blends books) to reinforce the sounds of the blends.
- Discuss the sounds made by these short vowels: 'a' — r*a*n, h*a*d, 'e' — g*e*t, R*e*d; 'i' — b*i*g, d*i*d; 'o' — fr*o*m, n*o*t; 'u' — n*u*t, r*u*n. Look for other words in the text.

Using the blackline master
- Have the children retell the story.
- Invite them to draw a matching picture.
- Encourage the children to look in their books for information to help them with their writing.

My name is _____

Draw a picture about the story.

Red Squirrel ran across the ground.

She _____.

Red Squirrel did not see the grey bird.

She _____.

A big grey bird was flying around.

He _____.

It was Red Squirrel's lucky day.

She _____.

RECOUNT

Running words: 140

The purpose of a recount is to retell the details of an event in sequential order. Letters and diaries are common forms of recounts. A recount is more personal than a report.

Feeding the Lambs

About the text
In this recount, Kate writes a letter to her gran and grandad about an enjoyable experience she had while visiting Sam's farm. This book further reinforces the non-fiction theme 'Food and eating'.

Linking with other PM books

The farm in spring	PM Library Starters Two
At the Toyshop	PM Plus N. F. Levels 5 & 6
It is Raining	PM Plus N. F. Levels 8 & 9
The waving sheep	PM Library Green Level

Creating the atmosphere

Reread *Baby Lambs first drink* (PM Library Red Level). Talk about caring for motherless lambs.

Focusing on the text

- **Cover** Read the title and discuss the cover photograph. Remind the children that lambs wag their tails when they are happy.

- **Page 2–3** Discuss the conventions of letter writing, i.e. setting out, opening and closing sentences, etc.

- **Pages 4–15** Notice that Kate's letter is personal and written in the past tense. Ask, 'Why is Kate writing a letter to her grandparents?' Point out that the events of the visit are recorded in a sequential order. Discuss how ideas have been grouped together. Talk about the features of report writing evident in Kate's letter.

- **Page 16** Discuss the recommendation made by Kate at the end of her letter. Read the letter with fluency and phrasing.

Going beyond the text

- Have the children pretend to be Gran or Grandad, replying to Kate's letter. Use the letter in the book as a model. Discuss what the children could write in their letters.

- Provide the children with card, cotton wool, scissors and glue. Have them make stand-up models of lambs. Add captions about caring for a young lamb.

- Discuss the illustrations in *The farm in spring*. Make a mural of a farm. Provide textured materials for the animals' coats. Attach descriptive captions to the mural.

- Write about how different animals use their tails.

> Cows swish their tails to keep flies and insects away. A Kangaroo's tail helps it to balance.

- Copy the poem 'I held a lamb' (*PM Library Story Books Teachers' Guide Green Level*, page 39) onto A5 pieces of paper. Give each child a copy to illustrate.

Developing specific skills
- Use the format of the text as a model for letter writing.
- Reinforce monitoring of past-tense verbs: saw, came, fed, drank, wagged.
- Read with fluency and phrasing.

Using the blackline master
- Reread the letter on page 16 of the text.
- Establish Kate's reason for writing. Discuss the possible content of Kate's thank-you letter. Record some of the children's ideas on a chart.
- Talk about pictures that the children could draw.

My name is _____

Dear Sam,

Thank you for letting me come to stay.

_____

_____

_____

_____

_____

Love from

_____

NON-FICTION LEVELS 14 & 15

EXPOSITORY

Running words: 173

An exposition presents an argument or states a firmly held position. Persuasive language is used to justify a point of view, with reasoning.

Healthy Food

About the text

A family's visit to a supermarket encourages children to think, reason, and express their knowledge and views about healthy food. This book further reinforces the non-fiction theme 'Food and eating'.

Linking with other PM books

Our Parents — PM Library N. F. Blue Level
Where Does Food Come From? — PM Plus N. F. Levels 14 & 15
Food is Fun — PM Plus N. F. Levels 14 & 15

Creating the atmosphere

Talk about healthy food. Write the children's ideas on a chart. Encourage them to give reasons to support their ideas.

Focusing on the text

- **Cover** Read the title together. Discuss the photograph and its setting.

- **Pages** 2–16 Discuss the content of this exposition, i.e. it is divided into parts with an opening statement, followed by information to support the opening statement, and ends with a photographic diagram summarising the authors' views.

— Encourage discussion as the children check the accuracy of the information in the text.

— Ensure that the children understand that the Healthy Food Pyramid on page 16 represents a simple visual concept of healthy food choices in an increasingly complex food market.

— Identify key statements. List the healthy food guidelines recommended by this text.

Going beyond the text

- Encourage the children to write and draw about their own experiences of shopping at a supermarket.

- With the children, write statements supporting the following sentence: 'Treat foods are fun to eat on special occasions.'

You can have treats to eat when it is your birthday. I had an ice cream cake. It was yummy. Abdul

- Make a collage of the Healthy Food Pyramid. Cut out appropriate pictures from food pamphlets or brochures.

- Visit the fruit and vegetable section of the local supermarket. Plan the visit together, e.g. seeking permission, making arrangements to get there, etc.

- Enlarge and copy the verse 'Growing Big and Strong' (see *Food is Fun*, page 16) onto card. Read and discuss the verse. Invite the children to add illustrations.

Developing specific skills

- Discuss the verbs often used when expressing an opinion: believe, think, agree, disagree.
- Use knowledge of oral language patterns when checking or confirming text structure.
- Talk about meaning reinforced by visual cues.

Using the blackline master

- Read the poem together and identify the missing words. Discuss the rhyming pattern.
- Demonstrate how to search the text for information to support each statement.
- Have the children explain what they will draw in the boxes.

My name is _____

Growing Big and Strong

We eat food that's good for us,
  so we grow big and _____.

If we are healthy, we can play
  and learn the whole day _____.

These vegetables are very good for us.

Fruit is very good for us and we all like it.

We must not eat a lot of **these** foods.

| PROCEDURAL | A procedural text gives sequential instructions about how to make or do something. |

Running words: 221

Making Party Food

About the text
The three recipes in this book will give children ideas for attractive party food that they can make. The recipes are child-centred in that the children will be able to do 95% of the preparation. All recipes contain healthy food.

Linking with other PM books
Making a Cat and a Mouse PM Plus N. F. Levels 5 & 6
Making a Caterpillar   PM Plus N. F. Levels 8 & 9
Making a Toy House   PM Plus N. F. Levels 11 & 12
Food is Fun   PM Plus N. F. Levels 14 & 15

Creating the atmosphere
Reread *A birthday cake for Ben* (PM Library Red Level). On a chart, list the procedures followed as the cake is made.

Focusing on the text
- **Cover** Read the title and identify the three party foods. Ensure that the children understand they are going to read recipes for making the three party foods. Encourage them to share their experiences of helping to cook.

- **Pages 2–16** Discuss the special features of this procedural text, i.e. bold headings, ingredients, procedures listed in sequential steps, helpful photographs. For each recipe:

— observe how the colour of paper changes

— read the name of the recipe and the materials and ingredients required to make it; predict what the instructions might be

— talk about tasks that adults would help with.

Going beyond the text
- Read the verses 'My Milk Shake' and 'Ice Cream' (see *Food is Fun*, pages 14–15). Compare the features of verse with procedural writing. Provide the children with copies of the verses and have them paste these into their personal anthologies.

- List tasks that the children do daily, e.g. clean their teeth, put on their socks and shoes, get ready for school, etc. Assist them to write and illustrate the procedures for some of these tasks.

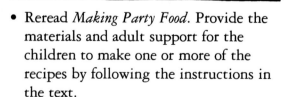

- Reread *Making Party Food*. Provide the materials and adult support for the children to make one or more of the recipes by following the instructions in the text.

Developing specific skills
- Identify the layout of a procedural text, i.e. materials required, lists, instructions or procedures, and the use of diagrams or photographs.
- Use a similar format to write procedures for tasks that are familiar to the children.

Using the blackline master
- Provide all the materials required. Have the children write and draw two extra fillings.
- Read the directions together.
- Discuss reasons why the children must wash their hands before handling food.

My name is _____

Making a sandwich

Ask your mum or dad or teacher to help you.

You will need:

bread   butter   egg   cheese

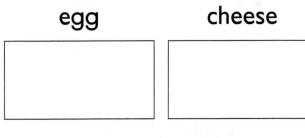

lettuce   tomato   _____ _____

1. Put some butter on the bread.

2. Put three things
   that you like on the bread.

3. Put some bread on top.

Now your sandwich is ready to eat.

My _____ helped me to make my sandwich.

Where Does Food Come From?

EXPLANATORY

Running words: 174

The purpose of an explanation is to define an idea or to explain cause and effect, e.g. 'Why does a lot of our food come from plants?'

Where Does Food Come From?

About the text

This scientifically accurate text explains how a lot of our food comes from plants. Clearly labelled diagrams and photographs inform the reader and encourage discussion about the continuing plant cycle.

Linking with other PM books

Sally's beans	PM Library Yellow Level
Look in the Garden	PM Plus Level 12
The Wheelbarrow Garden	PM Plus Level 14
Walking in the Summer	PM Library N. F. Green Level

Creating the atmosphere

Write the question, 'Where does food come from?' on a chart. Summarise the children's ideas and write them on the chart. Ask the children if they have any questions they are interested in solving about the topic. Write these on a chart.

Focusing on the text

- **Cover** Read the title and discuss the cover photographs. Explain that the information in the text is scientifically correct. Inform the children before they begin to read that they are not expected to read the labels.

- **Pages 2–16** Throughout the text:

— discuss the features of informative writing, i.e. key statements and related information

— observe the use of accurate photographs

— talk about how the information could be checked by finding similar information in other resources

— discuss the layout of the text, e.g. there are visual cues to help the reader with specialised vocabulary

— encourage the children to share their views on the continuing plant cycle.

Going beyond the text

- Read the questions that the children wished to find out about (see 'Creating the atmosphere'). Model how to present appropriate answers.

~ Does everything need food? ~
Every living thing has to have food to live.
Big animals, like elephants, need lots of food.
Small animals need very little food.

- Have the children 'mind-map' the key ideas.

- Individually, or in pairs, present information from the text on large charts. Discuss how to display key messages and diagrams. It is important that the children share their writing with others. Encourage them to evaluate how effectively the charts display essential information.

Developing specific skills

- Refer to key words and statements when retelling or summarising an explanation.
- Read silently for a purpose.
- Find and use relevant information from a variety of sources, e.g. books, pictures, CD-ROMs, etc.

Using the blackline master

- Demonstrate how to search the text to access information. Complete the first explanation together.
- Talk about explanations that the children might write about the other illustrations in the text.
- Discuss what they will draw in their pictures.

My name is _____

A lot of food comes from plants.

_____

_____

_____

_____

_____

_____

_____

_____

_____

Turn this page over.

Draw some more plants that you can eat.

REPORT

Running words: 210

A report describes a topic and is usually written in the present tense. It is an impersonal statement of fact, and may include observation.

Families and Feasts

About the text

This factual report describes special occasions and feasts celebrated by each of four families from different cultures. This book further reinforces the non-fiction theme 'Food and eating'.

Linking with other PM books

The Christmas tree	PM Library Blue Level
Birthday balloons	PM Library Blue Level
Birthday Presents	PM Plus Level 11
The Hospital Party	PM Plus Level 14

Creating the atmosphere

Study photographs of festive occasions from different cultures and countries. Discuss the excitement and reasons for these happy family gatherings.

Focusing on the text

- **Cover** Read the title together. Discuss the happy family gathering on the cover. Ask the children if they can identify the special foods depicted in the vignettes. Before the children read the text, explain that the book is about four different family occasions and feasts.

- **Pages 2–16** Throughout the text:

— read and discuss the events reported, and find the countries mentioned on a world map

— observe the happy family groups that are part of each special occasion

— discuss key words and demonstrate how to use these words when making a summary of each special occasion

— discuss the features of this observational report, i.e. selected occasions;

descriptive vocabulary with authentic settings, clothing, decorations, food and events enabling readers to learn from the text.

Going beyond the text

- Discuss the features of a report, i.e. opening statement, explanation or observation, and concluding statement. Assist the children to write a report about a recent school event.

> We are having a walkathon next week.
> On Wednesday, we will walk around the park. Our parents will come and watch.
> Each time we go around the park we will get a sticker.

- Make a list of festive occasions and how they are celebrated. Some children could add to the list by researching in the library or by asking at home.

- Revisit *On with the dance* (PM Library Readalongs). Read the text and practise the dances.

Developing specific skills

- Reinforce the factual recount of events in a report.
- Discuss the features of a report, i.e. opening statement, explanation, concluding statement.
- Check that the information in the text is supported by the accuracy of the visual information.

Using the blackline master

- Talk about the families and feasts reported in the text. Ask the children to write about one of these.
- Encourage them to share occasions when their own families gather together for a feast.
- Read the instructions together.

My name is _____

Look in *Families and Feasts.* Write about and draw a feast.

_____

_____

_____

_____

Write about a feast that you have been to.

_____

_____

_____

_____

VERSE

Verse is the rhythmic language that pleases the ear and stimulates the mind.

Food is Fun

About the text

This is a fun book of short verses that reinforce the enjoyment of eating good food. The verses may be read individually or in small groups. It is recommended that the teacher first read the verses to the children.

Linking with other PM books

Toys and Play	PM Plus N. F. Levels 5 & 6
The Sun, the Wind and the Rain	PM Plus N. F. Levels 8 & 9
Houses and Homes	PM Plus N. F. Levels 11 & 12

Creating the atmosphere

Allow the children to form their names with pasta letters. Talk about how these letters are sometimes placed in vegetable soup. Write the verse 'Alphabet Soup' (see page 4) on a chart. Read it together. Locate the words that rhyme.

Focusing on the text

The verses may be read over several days along with the other non-fiction books at the same level. Alternatively, all of the verses might be read in one guided-reading session. This choice suggests an in-depth study of the features of this type of writing.

- **Cover** Read the title together, and discuss the cover and title page illustrations.

- **Pages 2–16** Encourage the children to use visual information and their personal knowledge of how words work as they read the verses. Identify the special features of verse, e.g. text layout, rhyme, meaning and rhythmic language. Reinforce the enjoyment of reading this form of writing.

Developing specific skills

- Reinforce that verse has a different text layout.
- Listen to the sounds that rhyme and identify the letter patterns.
- Recite favourite verses from memory.
- Encourage the children to write their own verses.

Going beyond the text

- Invite the children to make copies of their favourite poems on the computer. Focus upon presentation techniques.

- Photocopy the verses from *Food is Fun* onto A5-sized paper. Ask the children to read and illustrate their favourites, before pasting them into their poetry anthologies.

- Enlarge each verse and paste it onto A3-sized cards. Have the children colour in the illustrations. Place the finished verses altogether in a box. Label the box 'Our Poems about Food'.

- Reread the verse 'Monkeys Eat Bananas' on page 10 of *Food is Fun*. Innovate upon the text by helping the children to write about other foods that are found up in trees.

Squirrels eat nuts
Way up in the tree.
Squirrels like nuts –
And so do we !

Using the blackline master

- Reread 'The Hungry Ants' on pages 12–13 of the text. Talk about other places where the ants might have gone. List the children's ideas on a chart.
- Read the position words in the boxes.
- Demonstrate where to write the position words. Ask the children to draw the ants and the objects in the boxes.

My name is _____

Read 'The Hungry Ants'.

Where do the ants go?

Here are some words to help you:

in	out	up	down	around	across	over

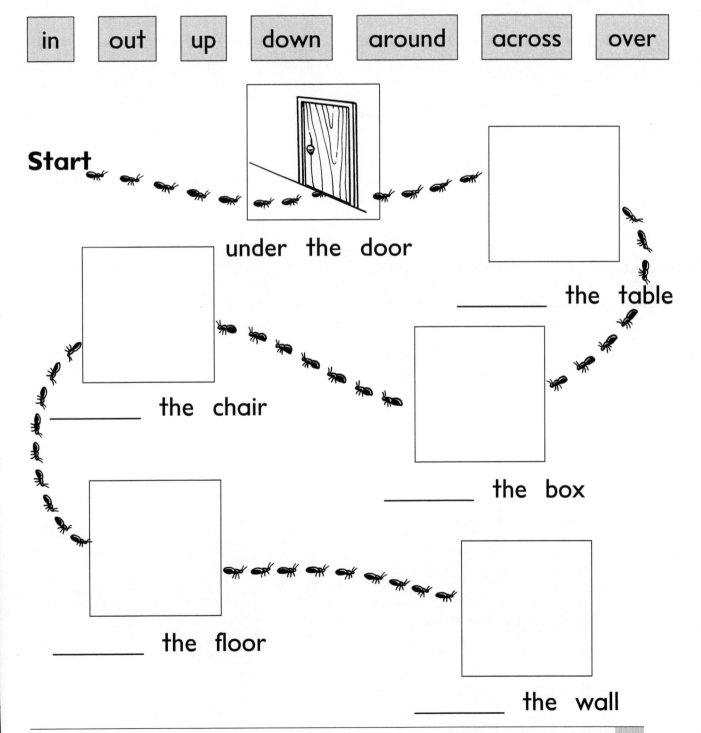

Start

under the door

_____ the table

_____ the chair

_____ the box

_____ the floor

_____ the wall

Language monitoring checks

Levels 12, 13 and 14
Skills, understandings and behaviours

									Date

Speaking and listening									
Speaks clearly and confidently on selected topics, maintaining the attention of the audience									
Clarifies or elaborates on ideas in response to questions									
Reading and writing									
Uses appropriate reading strategies more frequently									
Reads for meaning and understanding									
Displays confidence in taking risks and making approximations in reading and writing									
Displays more skill in reasoning and predicting									
Displays increasing independence in reading a variety of books									
Can read silently for a purpose									
Is developing expressive oral reading using punctuation									
Can discuss book characters, scenes and episodes with understanding									
Can spell many words correctly									
Makes logical attempts at spelling unknown words									
Is self-motivated to write often									
Is beginning to reread own writing for meaning and spelling accuracy									
Viewing and presenting									
Finds and uses information from a range of sources, e.g. books, pictures, videos									
Expresses feelings and ideas through different media, e.g. mime, movement, art, writing									

General comments (date all observations):

Reading record

Name: _____ **Age:** _____ **Date:** _____

Text: _The Donkey in the Lion's Skin_ **Level:** 12   **Running words:** 110

Summary: _____

_____

_____

Page		E	SC	Errors MSV	Self-corrections MSV
2	One day, a donkey saw a lion's skin in the long grass. "I have always wanted to be a lion," he said.				
4	The donkey got into the lion's skin. "I look like a lion now," he said, "and I am going to have some fun!" He went to hide in the long grass.				
6	Some zebras came along. The donkey jumped up, and ran after the zebras. "Help!" they cried. "A lion is coming to get us!" And they ran and ran.				
8	Then some foxes came along. The donkey jumped up, and ran after the foxes. "Help!" they cried. "A lion is coming to get us!" And they ran and ran.				
	Totals				

Reading record

Name: _____ **Age:** _____ **Date:** _____

Text: *The Classroom Caterpillars* **Level:** *13* **Running words:** *120*

Summary: _____

_____

_____

Page		E	SC	Errors MSV	Self-corrections MSV
2	On Friday morning, Katie came to school with a caterpillar in a box. She had some leaves in the box, too. Katie said to Miss Park, "I will look after this caterpillar. Can it stay here in our room?"				
4	"My caterpillar likes eating swan plant leaves," said Katie. Miss Park said, "Look under this leaf. Here are some little white eggs. Tiny caterpillars will come out of the eggs."				
6	On Monday morning, Katie came to school with a swan plant in a pot. "Look!" she said to Anna. "Some little caterpillars have come out of the eggs! They can eat this swan plant, too."				
8	All that week, and the next week, the tiny caterpillars nibbled at the swan plant leaves.				
	Totals				

Reading record • **Example:** *The Classroom Caterpillars* © Nelson, 2000.

Reading record

Name: _____ **Age:** _____ **Date:** _____

Text: _The Fawn in the Forest_ **Level:** _14_ **Running words:** _111_

Summary: _____

_____

_____

Page		E	SC	Errors MSV	Self-corrections MSV
2	A baby fawn lay hiding in the green forest.				
	He lay in the leaves and the long grass				
	under the trees.				
	He lay in a secret place.				
	His mother had hidden him there.				
4	The little fawn was all by himself.				
	He stayed very still.				
	The white spots on his back				
	looked like spots of sunlight on the leaves.				
6	A fox came along.				
	The baby fawn stayed very still.				
	He did not move his head.				
	He did not move his tail.				
7	The fox did not see the baby fawn,				
	and it walked past.				
8	A big cat came along.				
	The baby fawn did not move his ears.				
	He did not move his nose.				
	Totals				

Reading record

Name: _____   **Age:** _____   **Date:** _____

Text: _Healthy Food_ _____   **Level:** 14 & 15   **Running words:** 107 _____

Summary: _____

_____

_____

Page		E	SC	Errors MSV	Self-corrections MSV
2	We all need to eat food. We need to drink lots of water every day, too. Food helps children to grow and play, and to do their school work.				
4	Some foods are very good for us. We can eat lots of these foods.				
6	Vegetables are very good for us. We can eat them every day. Some vegetables are green and some are red. Some vegetables are white and some are orange.				
8	We can eat fruit every day. Apples and oranges and bananas are fruit. Fruit is very good for us.				
10	Children need to drink milk every day. Milk helps children to grow. Yoghurt is made from milk.				
	Totals				

Reading record

Name: _____ Age: _____ Date: _____

Text: _____ Level: _____ Running words: _____

Summary: _____

_____

_____

Page		E	SC	Errors MSV	Self-corrections MSV
	Totals				

PM Plus titles Levels 9–16

LEVEL 9

Story Books

Bugs for Breakfast
Sam Plays Swing Ball
The Beach House
Kitty Cat and the Paint
Baby Bear Climbs a Tree
Little Chimp and the Bees
The Fire on Toytown Hill
Brown Mouse Plays a Trick
Bingo Goes to School
Billy at School

LEVEL 10

Story Books

Baby Bear's Hiding Place
Sam's Painting
Lost Socks
Two Little Ducks Get Lost
Joe Makes a House
Brown Mouse Gets Some Corn
Little Chimp and Baby Chimp
Rabbits' Ears
The Swan Family
The House on the Hill

LEVEL 11

Story Books

Birthday Presents
Jack and Billy and Rose
Max and the Bird House
The Toytown Racing Car
The Best Hats
The Broken Flower Pot
Down by the Sea
A Treasure Island
Mother Tiger and her Cubs
Tom's Ride

LEVELS 11 & 12

Non-fiction

Our New House
Animal Homes
Our House is a Safe House
Making a Toy House
Building a House
Houses and Homes

LEVEL 12

Story Books

The Bears and the Magpie
A Friend for Max
Max and Jake
Snowball, the White Mouse
Look in the Garden
The Jungle Frogs
Jordan's Football
The Donkey in the Lion's Skin
The Lost Keys
The Picnic Boat

LEVEL 13

Story Books

Sam's Haircut
Little Chimp and the Termites
Three Little Mice in Trouble
The Crow and the Pot
New Glasses for Max
Lollipop, the Old Car
Locked In
Popcorn Fun
Coco's Bell
The Classroom Caterpillars

LEVEL 14

Story Books

The Hospital Party
Swimming with a Dragon
The Wheelbarrow Garden
Teasing Mum
Katie's Butterfly
The Nest on the Beach
The Fawn in the Forest
The Skipping Rope
A Tree Horse
Red Squirrel's Adventure

LEVELS 14 & 15

Non-fiction

Families and Feasts
Feeding the Lambs
Food is Fun
Healthy Food
Making Party Food
Where Does Food Come From?

LEVEL 15

Story Books

The Rocket Ship
The Blow-away Kite
The Little Blue Horse
Chooky
Look Out!
The Little Work Plane
A Bike for Alex
The Goats in the Turnip Field
Saving Hoppo
The Ant and the Dove

LEVEL 16

Story Books

The Mice Have a Meeting
The Big Bad Wolf
The Work Helicopter
The Youngest Giraffe
Swoop!
More Spaghetti!
The Lions and the Buffaloes
The Secret Cave
Jordan at the Big Game
The Triceratops and the
    Crocodiles

LEVELS 16 & 17

Non-fiction

Taking Care of Ourselves
Our Bodies
Living with Others
Games We Play
Our Clothes
Living and Growing

RUTLAND ELEMENTARY SCHOOL